Advance Praise for
The Contrarian Effect

"In sales as in life, it's not what you've been told to look for that matters, it's what you actually see for yourself. In this quick and entertaining look at all that is wrong with traditional sales tactics, Elizabeth and Michael give us wonderful examples of ways to see today's world of sales for what it really is: individuals seeking value in ways that matter personally. If you even just touch sales in your career (and whom among us does not) this book will open your eyes—and the view is great."

—Dan Roam, author of *The Back of the Napkin*

"I've made a career out of challenging conventional sales wisdom and I can tell you that very few writers have done this effectively. It's not demolition that's hard: anyone can say that everything you've ever read is wrong. The trick is building something better in its place. *The Contrarian Effect* does this well. It's filled with true stories about what works and what doesn't. It's fun to read and will challenge your thinking."

—Neil Rackham, author of *SPIN Selling*

"Want to know why traditional sales tactics suck? Customers resist them, salespeople hate using them, and they simply don't work. If you are ready to achieve incredible sales results, pick up a copy of *The Contrarian Effect* today!"

—Cali Ressler and Jody Thompson, authors of
Why Work Sucks and How to Fix It

"Truth. Honesty. Dignity. Respect. Four words not often heard in the world of sales. In this remarkable little book, Michael and Liz offer real insight and practical advice on how to truly satisfy customers—the key to success in every sale. Bravo!"

—Keith Ferrazzi, bestselling author of
Never Eat Alone

"*The Contrarian Effect* replaces conventional sales wisdom with new strategies that actually work in today's business climate. You'll achieve far greater sales success with much less effort."

—Jill Konrath, author of *Selling to Big Companies*
and CEO of SellingtoBigCompanies.com

Contrarian

THE CONTRARIAN EFFECT

Why It Pays (Big) to Take Typical Sales
Advice and Do the Opposite

Michael Port
and Elizabeth Marshall

WILEY
John Wiley & Sons, Inc.

Published by John Wiley & Sons, Inc., Hoboken, New Jersey
Published simultaneously in Canada

For general information on our other products and services or for technical support, please
contact our Customer Care Department within the United States at (800) 762-2974,
outside the United States at (317) 572-3993 or fax (317) 572-4002.

Wiley also publishes its books in a variety of electronic formats. Some content that
appears in print may not be available in electronic books. For more information about
Wiley products, visit our web site at www.wiley.com.

Library of Congress Cataloging-in-Publication Data:

Port, Michael, 1970-
    The contrarian effect : why it pays (big) to take typical sales advice and do the
opposite / Michael Port and Elizabeth Marshall.
        p.   cm.
    Includes bibliographical references and index.
    ISBN 978-0-470-23790-8 (cloth)
        1. Selling.   2. Sales management.   3. Marketing.   I. Marshall,
Elizabeth, 1975-   II. Title.
HF5438.25.P673   2008
658.8'02—dc22

                                                                2008014657

Printed in the United States of America

10 9 8 7 6 5 4 3 2 1

Contents

Section 4: May Cause Headaches, Dizziness, and Internal Bleeding

Acknowledgments

―――――――― ∾ ――――――――

THE CONTRARIAN EFFECT is a beautiful example of what can happen when you collaborate with others and choose to leverage the wisdom and experience of others. It symbolizes the collective efforts of a wonderful community of people—incredible souls that Michael and Elizabeth are honored to know. In that spirit, we wish to express our deepest gratitude and thanks:

To Kathy Green, Michael's agent, for her willingness and desire to support this book and this message.

To Matt Holt and the entire team at John Wiley & Sons, Inc. for your wisdom, expertise, and support. Thank you for the work you do to spread the message of business authors and experts like us.

To our R&D Team, who dedicated their time and talents to this project: Krista Baker, Chris Smude, Liz Kruz-Kaegi, Christopher Bates, Lori Richardson, Merrily Sable, Jade Barclay, and Sarah Robinson. Thank you for your willingness to conduct and compile research for our thesis and to provide your experience and expertise as we honed and refined the message. Special thanks to Krista Baker for digging up several great examples we were able to include in the final draft and to Cara Lumen for your excellent suggestions and observations. Additional thanks to Hugh Strickland, Susan Kim, and Rob Thomas for reading the draft and providing insightful comments and suggestions. Last but not least, big thanks to Michael Stammer, our colleague and friend, for his valuable insights and years of sales experience that helped shape the ideas and the concepts in this book.

To Sharon Dawson, Elizabeth's mom, for her gift with words and her love of grammar. Thank you for editing the draft and for making sure we articulated our ideas in the best way possible.

To Starbucks manager Andy Whisenhunt and the entire staff of the Starbucks #6262 in Dallas, Texas, who let Elizabeth camp out for hours on end as she wrote and edited the book. They are an example of a team that goes above and beyond on a daily basis. Additional thanks to Tom, Terri, Steve, Jennifer, Amy, Carrie, Glenn, Ray, and the rest of the "Starbucks Gang" for your continual support, ideas, and suggestions.

To Gayla DeHart, who inspires us with her brilliance and supports us with her invaluable friendship.

To the entire team at Book Yourself Solid, Linsey Card, Becky Wingate, and Katherine Bellefontaine, who provide unfailing support and who stand behind us in both small and big ways. Thank you for your devotion and commitment to our clients and mission.

To all the clients of Book Yourself Solid and members of the Think Big Revolution. Your energy, creativity, and talents keep us committed to thinking bigger about who we are and what we offer the world.

To all our friends and colleagues that we regret we cannot list out individually. Deepest thanks for supporting our message. We couldn't do this work without you.

To all the salespeople out there that ever tried to pitch us something. Thank you for giving us real-world examples and experiences that support the concepts and strategies in this book.

To companies like Southwest Airlines, Starbucks, Apple, Amazon, Cabela's, Costco, and many other organizations that embody the principles and the practices we preach. You demonstrate why it pays to take the typical sales advice and do the opposite. Thank you for modeling that making the shift is not only possible, but highly profitable.

Finally, to sales professionals like you, who already believe in payoff and value of the Contrarian Effect. Thank you for being a change agent and for being a leader—one that others can aspire to follow.

From the Old World to the New

———————— ≈ ————————

IN 1907, CAPTAIN EDWARD JOHN SMITH was at the height of his career.

A highly respected sea captain, a commander in the Royal Naval Reserve, and commodore of the White Star Fleet, Captain Smith knew a thing or two about how to sail a ship. With a successful track record and a career spanning more than four decades, it's understandable that

White Star asked Smith to command the company's newest ships on their maiden voyages.

Upon arriving in New York after the maiden voyage of the *Adriatic* in May 1907, Captain Smith was interviewed about his 40 years of experience at sea (from www .TitanicStory.com):

───────────────── ≈ ─────────────────

When anyone asks how I can best describe my experience in nearly 40 years at sea, I merely say, uneventful. Of course there have been winter gales, and storms and fog the like, but in all my experience, I have never been in any accident of any sort worth speaking about. I never saw a wreck and never have been wrecked, nor was I ever in any predicament that threatened to end in disaster of any sort.

────────────────────────────────────

Given his knowledge, his expertise, and his understanding at the time, Captain Smith would have considered the tragic disaster that culminated in the sinking of the *Titanic* five years later a near impossibility. He made that clear. In fact, Captain Smith also said, "I cannot imagine any condition which would cause a ship to founder. I cannot conceive of any vital disaster happening to this vessel. Modern shipbuilding has gone beyond that."

One year before setting sail, *Shipbuilder* magazine described the *Titanic* as "practically unsinkable," with state-of-the-art construction and watertight doors. With its beautiful design and elegant decor, it was one that every captain wanted to sail and every traveler wanted to experience. Therefore, it seemed fitting that Captain Smith chose to end his career in 1912 by leading the line's newest ship, the *Titanic,* to sea.

Sadly, Captain Smith and the ship's officers in charge of steering the mighty boat had multiple opportunities to change course to avoid the 78 miles of ice they smacked into. The *Titanic* received over seven warnings throughout the course of the day, alerting them to the large mass of ice directly in their path. Perhaps the ship's officers did not recognize or heed the warnings in light of the opportunity ahead of them: beating the speed record of its sister ship, the *Olympus,* by reaching New York City on Tuesday night. In fact, the chief engineer advised Captain Smith that by lighting four additional boilers, the ship could reach a maximum speed of 22 knots.

Despite the warnings, the ship's officers were not concerned. As a result, they neglected to deliver a few of the warnings throughout the day to Captain Smith. After all, ice was common in the North Atlantic in April, and the ship's officers felt they could see and avoid an iceberg in plenty of time. Captain Smith considered the ice warnings to be insignificant and irrelevant enough that he retired for the evening at 9:20 P.M. and left the ship's care to Second Officer Herbert Lightoller.

Captain Smith's false certainty cost him his life and the lives of over 1,500 people.

Ironically, Captain Smith couldn't seem to accept the possibility of such a crash, even though writers like Morgan Robertson and William T. Stead had conceived of the exact circumstances that sank the ship. Fourteen years prior to the *Titanic*'s first—and final—voyage, Robertson wrote a fictitious tale about the *Titan,* a mighty ship that hit an iceberg in the Atlantic Ocean on a cold April night. Sound familiar? Although Robertson's novel was a work of fiction, the designs of the *Titan* and the actual *Titanic* were strikingly similar, as were their fates. Similarly, English journalist William T. Stead published a novel in 1892, *From the Old World to the New,* in which he described the sinking of a ship in the North Atlantic after hitting an iceberg. Although Stead's ship was called the *Majestic,* the ship's captain was named Edward J. Smith, the same name of the actual captain of the *Titanic.* Strangely, William T. Stead was aboard the *Titanic*'s maiden voyage and lost his life at sea—under the exact same circumstances he had conceived in his novel and in an 1886 article in the *Pall Mall Gazette,* titled "Futility."

Obviously, no one would have expected Captain Smith to take his cues from a work of fiction. Yet it is very clear after the fact that Smith missed several clues in the years, months, days, and even hours before the tragedy. Given the multitude of signals, it seems possible that he couldn't even see what was happening or was too distracted by the opportunity to beat the speed record held by the *Olympus*. Perhaps he couldn't imagine something he had not experienced—despite articles, novels, and stories that described such a possibility. Or perhaps he was not open to the possibility that shifts in reality are indeed possible.

What is important to note is not why Captain Smith missed the signs but that he did. That error was a fatal one, impacting the lives of the passengers, the ship's officers, and the families that waited in vain for their safe arrival home.

Sign of the Times

Like Captain Smith, many sales professionals are missing the signs. Although missing the signs won't cost you your life, they will impact you—and result in lost sales, damaged relationships, stress, and fatigue. There are signals all around us indicating that the market has changed and that the typical sales tactics—cold calling, door-to-door selling, closing questions, sales scripts, and the like—are broken.

Perhaps a customer complaint or the loss of what was previously a shoe-in account has got you thinking about what it *really* takes to be successful in sales. Maybe you've noticed that it takes more and more energy to reach fewer and fewer potential clients using the traditional tactics, or you've felt more and more pressure from executives and your VP to continue to increase your sales.

Perhaps you've grown tired of the endless search for new prospects that is inevitable when you focus on the short-term success over building long-term relationships. Perhaps you are sick of the hang-up calls and the do-not-call restrictions that block you from reaching new prospects. Or possibly the pressure to close sales and convince clients to sign on the dotted line before they are ready just so you can "make quota" has gotten old. And maybe, just maybe, you are not so comfortable with the "way things are done in sales." It's starting to turn off potential customers, customers who seem to pass judgment on you because they're fed up with the typical tactics and assume that you use them like everyone else.

Your potential customers still equate selling with the typical tactics, whether you practice them or not. Customers are all too aware of the most common ways that sales professionals purportedly use to capture their attention and close the deal—which often means that sales professionals are guilty until proven innocent. Not only are they familiar with these methods, they have come to expect them as part of the sales process.

This is understandable, given that many of the typical tactics and strategies—elements of the traditional sales process—came into existence long before the *Titanic* set sail.

According to Harvard professor and author Walter A. Friedman, one man in particular is primarily responsible for developing and popularizing many of the selling techniques that are still in existence today.

Birth of a Salesman

As the founder of National Cash Register (NCR), John H. Patterson created a detailed system to monitor and train company salesmen. With the help of his brother-in-law, Joseph Crane, he established the first sales training school on company grounds. One of the most significant elements of the sales training program was the sales script Crane wrote, which eventually developed into the *NCR Primer* in 1887. The *Primer* was a comprehensive training manual that told sales professionals what to say and how to say it, how to navigate through the four stages in every sale, and how to close the customer and sell a cash register.

Patterson's method was detailed, yet efficient. He taught his salesmen many skills, including how to:

- Overcome objections
- Rid their sales territory of any competition
- Assume the sale in order to convince prospects to buy
- Sell within a framework of sales quotas and commission incentives

With the help of the *Primer,* Patterson instructed salesmen to exert pressure in a forceful, yet subtle, manner in order to make sales. The *Primer* illustrated a number of closing techniques, such as the following:

After you have made your proposition clear and feel sure that the merchant realizes the value of the register, do not ask for an order, take for granted that he will buy. Say to him "Mr. Blank, what color shall I make it?" or "How soon do you want delivery?" Take out your order blank, fill it out, and handing him your pen, say, "Just sign where I have made the cross."

Patterson was not the first to use scripts. In 1859, the Equitable Life Assurance Society published a document, *Hints for Agents,* so that company salesmen would have a list of persuasive arguments to use with potential customers. But Patterson was the best in implementing a comprehensive and systematic way to train sales professionals and show them exactly what to do to sell. In studying the influence of Patterson, Friedman explains, "Not only is study of Patterson's leadership style informative and interesting, but a review of his foundations of modern sales techniques reveals a long list of familiar terms and methods that illuminates current practice."

Patterson's method certainly seemed to work. During the period from 1888 to 1895, approximately 84 companies sold cash registers and competed with NCR for business. Only three of those 84 competitors stayed in business for any length of time—mainly because Patterson did everything he could to squash the competition. Fiercely competitive, he sued many of the companies that made premium registers and put many of them out of business. Patterson employed every competitive tactic and called upon every law he could to stay ahead of the competition, which included suing Heintz Cash Register for patent infringement and buying up the inventory of Hallwood Company so that it could not meet customer demands. By 1912, NCR had captured 95 percent of the market—but not without consequence. The following year, the United States Grand Jury found Patterson and NCR guilty of violating antitrust laws.

Perhaps Patterson's success was a combination of both his efficient and comprehensive sales training system and his willingness to use deceptive sales tactics to outsell the competition. Sometimes, mere persuasion and effective use of closing questions would close the sale. At other times, more drastic measures were necessary. In an 1892 internal company memo, he instructed his sales force on how to demonstrate the "faulty" construction of a competitor's machine to potential customers as a way to sell more cash registers. Patterson believed that "to succeed in business, it is necessary to make others see things as you see them."

Patterson's stamp on many of the current-day selling techniques is clear. His sales philosophy and sales system not only impacted the development of modern-day selling but shaped the growth of many businesses during the early 1900s and for years thereafter.

Patterson's methods, along with the theories of other business leaders during his time, helped create what we now know as the traditional selling process and the traditional sales tactics. This means that the average sales professional indoctrinated in this method tends to approach selling from this viewpoint:

- Cold calling is an effective way to generate leads, since everyone is a potential customer.
- Prospecting means that you make a certain number of calls each day (usually 100) in order to reach potential clients.
- The numbers game is a tried-and-true formula that helps sales professionals determine how many calls they have to make in order to set a certain number of meetings and to make a certain number of sales.

- Canned or scripted presentations are effective, since most potential clients have the same needs and desires.

- During a potential-client meeting, the sales professional's job is to present the product or service, explain the features and benefits, handle any customer objections, and then close the sale.

- Tactics such as closing techniques and other strategies used to speed up the sale are vital, since it's critical for sales professionals to "make their numbers."

We're Not in Kansas Anymore

Despite massive changes in technology, communication, and innovation, as well as shifts in business and commerce over the past 100 years, many companies still adhere to the original selling practices first developed by John H. Patterson, with the hope that these practices will produce sales in the same way that they did for NCR and its sales force.

Is that a realistic expectation, however, and does it make sales sense?

While Patterson's methods certainly seemed effective in increasing sales and training salesmen around the turn of the century, are they a fit for today's sales professional? After all, the conditions and circumstances that Patterson's sales team experienced in selling cash registers are radically different from today's environment and market. It's a market in which customers do not tolerate self-serving behavior or tactics meant to speed up the sale or benefit the sales professional at the expense of the customer. Unlike Patterson's era, one in which the company could control who had access to information and details about its products and services, today's market gives potential clients access to unlimited information and the power to choose and control their reality. Your customers can dig up everything about you and your company—before you even open your mouth—by talking to the vendors, distributors, manufacturers, strategic partners, and anyone who has even done business with you.

Caution: You're in the No-Spin Sales Zone

Like the signals that Captain Smith received in the hours before the *Titanic* crash, the signs indicating a market shift are everywhere—consistent and frequent reminders that the old way doesn't work anymore. In fact, there are at least eight major signs pointing to shifts in the market and the manner in which customers want you to interact with them:

1. *Customers find you and initiate the buying process—not the other way around.*

    Today, customers initiate the buying process, evaluate whether they want what you have to offer, and then raise their hands when they want to buy. Instead of your trying to sell them, they want to be in control and they want to manage that process.

This means that sales professionals must find a way to build relationships and to be there when customers are ready to buy—a totally different worldview and way of interacting with potential customers. Something that won't be possible if you insist on selling to them and use the usual approach to reach and communicate with them.

2. *Customers are in control of how—and if—you reach and communicate with them.*

Prospecting, the act of seeking out potential customers, is not what it used to be. With one click of a button, today's customer can declare you irrelevant. Consumers have complete control and the ability to screen out any unwanted offers or outdated sales pitches. With customer-centered laws like the Do Not Call Registry and CAN-SPAM Act, your chances of successfully cold-calling or soliciting strangers are virtually zero. Even businesses have a way of filtering out unwanted solicitations. No elevator pitch or cold-calling script is going to help you reach them if they hang up or click Delete before you have the opportunity to describe what you offer.

Many elements of the traditional sales process are not aligned with the current environment and with customers' wishes and needs. Specifically, your customers' buying cycles are always out of sync with your sales cycle. When you cold-call and interrupt potential clients in order to follow your selling process, you have little or no chance of winning their attention and earning the right to keep in touch with them. Why? You are selling to them when they are not ready or interested in buying.

3. *Customers have unlimited choices and access to unlimited information.*

Your customers sit in the catbird seat. With seemingly infinite choices about what to buy and where to buy it, they can be ultraselective and extra careful about who they let into their world. Before deciding to move ahead, they can learn anything and everything about your product or service—and dig up information about you.

As a result, they have little tolerance for sales professionals who:

- Persuade them to buy something other than *exactly* what they want
- Attempt to hide or cover up shortcomings and weaknesses in their product or service
- Use closing questions or other pressure tactics to scare them into buying on their timetable

- Believe in anything other than radical transparency, honesty, and integrity

When sales professionals employ the old strategies designed to speed up the timing of the sale and close the deal in order to reach their sales goals, customers simply walk away. They can quickly and easily find someone else who won't pressure them into buying or withhold information from them.

4. *Customers are looking for you in new ways.*

Once potential clients decide that they are in need of your product or service, they tend to do one of two things: They either do a Google search to find what they're looking for or they ask their friends for a recommendation about whom to contact. They don't check their e-mail, listen to their voice messages, or sift through their junk mail to find you. Even if they are interested in learning more about you, they don't want to receive a cold call or unsolicited e-mail. They want to find you in the way they want to search for you—online and among people they trust.

5. *Customers want a relevant and valuable offer tailored just for them.*

Mass marketing and generic sales pitches are out. Communicating with individual customers is in.

Customers know when you haven't done your research or when you use the same sales shtick with everyone you meet. Since your potential clients won't stand for anything less than a tailored offer and customized communication, the older forms of reaching customers, such as cold calling, fall on deaf ears. Clients want—and can demand—relevant, authentic, timely, and engaging offers that are created just for them. In order to accommodate them, you must step back from the traditional way of reaching them and find a way that's more in touch and in step with them.

6. *Customers decide when it's time to buy—not you.*

Because customers have access to all types of information on the Web and talk to other consumers, they know all about your quotas, your sales goals, and the pressure you face each and every month to close deals. They've got the inside scoop—and they're not falling prey to pressure-filled selling processes any longer. They won't be persuaded to buy before they are ready or buy just to help you make your numbers. In their experience, the traditional sales approach is all about the sales professional and is not in sync with their timing or with what's best for them.

7. *Customers demand respect—and carry a big megaphone.*

Before the Internet and Web 2.0, customers were more willing to tolerate bad behavior from sales professionals, mainly because they had far fewer options, much less power than they do now, and almost no recourse to fight back in a way that made a difference. Those days are gone. Now, customers insist on being treated with equality and respect. Respect that amounts to more than just a friendly smile and an attempt at sincerity. They want the sales professional to recognize and acknowledge their right to do business with *anyone* they choose, and they want sales professionals to communicate with them according to their rules.

In no uncertain terms, they want you to:

- Listen to them and actually do what they ask you to do
- Keep your commitments to them
- Let them tell you what they want and what is best for them
- Allow them to decide when it's the right time to buy

If you treat customers with disrespect, lie to them, or pressure them to buy before they are ready, they now have enough power to fight back effectively. Consumers can publish their experiences in mere seconds through blog posts or via online forums. They can rapidly and successfully spread the word about their negative encounters, wreaking havoc on you and your reputation.

If you employ the traditional selling methods, chances are good that your potential customers will react negatively and let others know about their experience, which results not only in one lost sale but in many lost sales and a tarnished reputation.

8. *Customers don't trust you until you prove that you're worthy of their trust.*

While your customers have access to more information than ever before, they are also more skeptical than in years past. They are less likely to take what they see or hear at face value and don't automatically trust that you have their best interests in mind—thanks to scandals like Enron and the subprime mortgage crisis.

If you do anything other than respect their power to choose and take steps to earn their trust, you're off the list. It takes more than a catchy sales pitch and a closing question or two to earn the right to be in a relationship with them. They want you to demonstrate that you care about their needs, that you tell an authentic story, and that you are willing to build trust and credibility with them over time—giving them an opportunity to know, like, and trust you. Customers get to decide the speed of the sales cycle, which is why many of the old-school strategies repel customers and don't succeed in building the trust needed for customers to buy from you again and again and again.

These eight important indicators around you clearly point to an irreversible sea change and illustrate four significant reasons why the traditional sales strategies are broken and are no longer effective tools to build relationships and generate sales:

1. Many typical tactics are irrelevant, outdated, and out of sync with today's customer and today's market.
2. Many typical tactics are designed to benefit the salesperson rather than—and often at the expense of—the customer.
3. While many typical tactics appear to generate immediate results, they damage relationships and hinder long-term sales success.
4. Many typical tactics harm reputations and create negative unintended consequences, which often outweigh the immediate or short-term benefit of using the tactics.

The time to change directions is yesterday. Hoping the market will become less crowded or that customers will magically welcome the old-school strategies again is akin to Captain Smith wishing the iceberg out of existence. It's time to recognize the signs and to change course before you, your company, or your industry collides with a massive iceberg of customer resistance.

Follow the Leader

Instead of fighting the shift and resisting what *is,* you and your company have an incredible opportunity to make an immediate course correction. You have the potential to be wildly successful by embracing a radically different approach to reach customers, to increase sales, and to generate word-of-mouth buzz, the consequence of which will be nothing short of revolutionary. Starting today, you can adopt new strategies and create what we call the "Contrarian Effect."

It's easier than you think—requiring less effort, less energy, and less money than you're expending right now. In fact, many companies and sales professionals, maybe your competition, have already made the shift.

Want to know what's possible when you adopt the contrarian approach instead of the "always be closing" strategy? Just ask Apple. Apple's sales associates create a low-pressure, fun, and stimulating environment that opens doors and invites customers to buy when they are ready. As a result, Apple doesn't have to ask for the sale. By focusing on opening doors and building relationships, customers come to the company and stop in one of its stores on a Sunday afternoon to learn more about the latest and greatest products—or even to sit in on a free class. Because Apple always has free events and something of value to offer prospects, the company can quickly build trust and credibility and follow up with potential clients without asking for the sale or pressuring them to buy.

Cabela's, an outdoor retailer, also demonstrates how profitable it can be to take the contrarian approach and implement the "always be opening" strategy. Known for its friendly sales force and extremely knowledgeable staff, customers flock to Cabela's on a regular basis to check out new products and to hang out in the store. But that's just one of the ways that Cabela's has taken the contrarian approach.

Instead of using traditional sales scripts and standard FAQ product sheets, Cabela's employees create the Contrarian Effect by communicating with potential customers in a relaxed and conversational way. That's because Cabela's allows its sales associates to test out products in order to better understand and answer the questions a customer might ask. By putting a loaner program in place, Cabela's not only gives its sales force a chance to speak from experience instead of from a script, but helps them to step into the shoes of potential customers and to see things from their perspective. The company has chosen to stop pushing and to listen to what customers want and how to best serve them.

Want to know what's possible when you keep your promises and respect your customers? Just ask USAA (United Services Automobile Association). According to a 2007 survey conducted by *Business Week*, "Ninety-six percent of home and 98 percent of auto policyholders report that USAA meets their commitments to call back regarding claim issues on time." As a result of its ability to make and fulfill commitments, over 79 percent of USAA customers are willing to recommend its services to colleagues and friends. By treating customers in the best way possible, USAA not only opens doors but also builds trust and credibility with potential customers through an enthusiastic referral base of existing clients. A great move, since most potential clients are asking business associates and family members about where to buy and who is worthy of their trust.

Want to know what's possible when you do the opposite of interrupting customers with generic pitches? Just ask Amazon. This ultrasuccessful online bookstore understands the importance of making relevant and customized offers. By taking steps to understand its customers' interests and preferences, Amazon can follow up with recommendations and suggestions that are in sync with its customers. Amazon knows if you are a dog enthusiast or a sports fanatic. It knows if you are more likely to buy business books than romance novels. In short, the company understands—and listens to—its customers in order to make tailored and relevant offers.

Each one of these companies shows you what's possible when you take the typical sales advice and do the opposite.

For Your Consideration

As you read this book, consider whether the strategies and techniques you may currently rely on for sales success are the best ways to reach customers, win sales, and earn your piece of the market. Consider whether what you *think* makes sales sense may make no sense at all. Consider whether there's another way . . . or many other ways.

The Contrarian Effect is for all the sales professionals, sales managers, and companies who are interested in discovering better and more effective ways to sell more, to rise to the top of their industry, and to be remarkable.

Specifically, this book is for sales professionals who:

- Suspect or even know that their old selling methods no longer work
- Want to do more than just "make their numbers" and get by

- Desire to become the best for their clients, for their company, and for themselves
- Want to find a smarter, easier, and more effective way to build relationships and to sell

It's also for sales managers and companies who:

- Want new and better ways to help their sales teams produce, build relationships, and generate repeat business
- Desire long-term success—more than just the quick win or immediate sale
- Want to ensure that they are using the best and most effective strategies to attract and retain customers
- Know that the success of Apple, Southwest Airlines, Amazon, and others is something they can achieve, too—but only if they change the way they're currently doing things

It is our intention to show you throughout the course of this book why it pays—and pays big—to take the typical sales advice and do the opposite.

Section 1

Two Left Feet

~

*Typical Tactics Are
Out of Sync with the Market*

RELEVANCE IN SALES MATTERS. I's the difference between an open door and a shut one. Between a friendly greeting and the sound of a dial tone in your ear. Between a request for more information and a conversation killer, such as "We're not interested, but thanks anyway."

What does *relevance* mean? Relevance is relation to the matter at hand. It means that you have practical and social applicability. For sales professionals, relevance means that you are timely, current, and in sync with your market and your environment. Just ask Apple.

The Biggest Loser

When Apple required its iPhone customers to use AT&T to power the phone, both Apple and AT&T lost revenue and sales as a result of irrelevance.

In the months before the official launch of the iPhone, Apple fans and tech geeks alike eagerly awaited the day on which they could purchase the slick new device. During the waiting period, cell phone companies scrapped and fought for the opportunity to be the company to power Apple's new toy. In the end AT&T won the prize: the exclusive right to provide phone and data service for the iPhone.

Many customers who bought the iPhone didn't appreciate the exclusivity of this pairing.

As a result, they took steps to unlock the iPhone immediately after purchasing it in order to break away from AT&T. Customers who did sent a clear and direct message to Apple: that AT&T's service plan is not a relevant—or wanted—addition to the way-cool iPhone I just bought. Instead of putting up with this arrangement, they took matters into their own hands and found other cell phone service providers to work with the phone.

Although the exact number of unlocked iPhones is unclear, Toni Sacconaghi of Bernstein Research estimates that there may be as many as 1.4 million of them. It's hard to say, since some of those 1.4 million phones may be sitting on store shelves. In any event, there's a gap between the total number of iPhones sold by Apple (approximately 4 million) and the number of iPhones activated with AT&T (approximately 2 million). That gap translates into millions of lost dollars for AT&T—and for Apple, which makes a commission on each new AT&T customer who signs up.

Steve Jobs took a step toward irrelevance, and Apple missed the mark by insisting that its customers use the AT&T service. Instead of allowing customers the flexibility and option to choose their own phone provider, Apple made an uncharacteristic move, a decision that made it difficult for international users to purchase cell phone coverage for their iPhones and that created a barrier for U.S. customers who didn't want to pay cell phone cancellation charges to switch to AT&T just to own an iPhone.

Some estimate that Apple lost millions in revenue because it teamed up with AT&T. Others dispute that figure, pointing to AT&T as the bigger loser. After all, Apple still makes money from sales of the phone itself, regardless of whether customers stick with AT&T or attempt to unlock the device. But without a "cooperative" customer who follows the rules, AT&T loses out, both in lost subscribers and lost revenue.

Your prospects do care about relevance. They aren't concerned about the hoops you have to jump through to be timely, current, and in sync with their needs and desires. But they do require it if you want to build a relationship with them—and profit from that relationship. Because being relevant is about the only thing that will cut through the endless offers and solicitations they receive.

Pitches, Pitches, Everywhere

Right now, your prospects and potential clients are on the receiving end of over 5,000 ads, sales pitches, and marketing messages each day, according to Yankelovich, a market research firm. Consumers who live in metropolitan areas can hardly step out of their houses without coming into contact with ads or solicitations. Ads are ubiquitous, lining the backs of bathroom stalls, the walls of subway and bus stations, and the halls of every major airport. They spill out of every form of print media and pop up on just about every page we surf on the Web. In a *New York Times* article titled, "Anywhere the Eye Can See, It's Likely to See an Ad," writer Louise Story reports that even motion sickness bags on airplanes are now coveted ad spaces.

As a result of advertising overload, your prospects now have a shorter attention span, a tendency to jump from one source of stimulation to another, and a limited ability and willingness to listen to what you have to offer. If you combine the shortened attention span with the endless amount of options available to them and the ability to tune out, delete, ignore, or filter out your attempts to reach them, it becomes clear that the playing field has changed.

Companies and sales departments with deep pockets no longer control how buyers consume their messages. Customers do. In this new reality, attention is the new currency and your customers control what they watch, read, and hear. The shift in power from company to consumer is one of the key findings that Ketchum, a public relations firm and communications leader, discovered as part of a 2007 survey that polled over 1,200 U.S. consumers. As Ketchum senior vice president Nicholas Scibetta explains, "The survey results also show that today, more than ever, each consumer can search out the specific information he or she is seeking while tuning out the media sources that aren't personally relevant or meaningful."

Thanks to TiVo, Caller ID, and the delete button, your customers no longer have to endure or tolerate anything that isn't exactly what they want. While some customers are not always clear about what they want, they *do* know when your offer is irrelevant or off the mark.

Not only can they ignore you, but they feel empowered to push back anytime your pitch becomes too frequent or too much—a sobering fact that makes using the traditional sales process a major liability, since it was not created with this new reality in mind.

Although out-of-sync offers tend to be the norm, you might have a very hard time reaching some people using the typical tactics, in spite of having a great opportunity for them. For instance, if you are a salesperson at a medical recruiting company, you are in the business of finding relevant and highly qualified physicians to fill positions for your clients (often large hospitals). To do so, your daily routine goes something like this: Make 100 calls a day to a targeted list of physicians in an attempt to find qualified candidates interested in and open to interviewing for the positions offered on behalf of their clients.

The task sounds simple, and the formula for success seems clear—at least in theory.

Often, however, these targeted lists really aren't so targeted. Sure, all names on the list may be physicians rather than Australian shepherd breeders, which certainly helps. Then what? Just being a physician doesn't make the candidate ideal for the job you're offering.

What happens, then, when the doctors on the list aren't interested? What if they found a job three years ago and complain to you that they've repeatedly asked to be taken off the list? What if they are retired or unqualified due to malpractice claims? What if they've had a terrible experience with the company and never want to hear from you again?

Unless you know what's relevant to the prospects on the list, making cold calls is a bit like playing Russian roulette. You're always running the risk of being outdated, irrelevant, and unwanted.

After receiving an irrelevant offer, prospects will most likely screen you out. They can do that in a number of ways: by joining the Do Not Call list, by asking you to take them off your list, and by blocking your phone number so that you can never reach them again.

Even with this market shift, many organizations still continue to use cold calling as a primary sales tactic. They continue to use it without permission from the prospect and without stopping to ask whether their offer makes sense. They continue to use it without understanding that what was relevant last month (or last week) is not necessarily relevant today. And they continue to use it without noticing that the prospect has moved on to something else.

So, if the typical tactics such as cold calling are both outdated (because they can be blocked) and irrelevant (because they are unsolicited and unwanted), then why do sales professionals insist on using them? We tend to stick with what's expected and go with what we know—because it's safe and easy. We tend to do what's traditional, even when it's no longer effective.

Mother May I?

Sales professionals and companies can quickly get back in sync with their prospects' needs and desires by adopting several contrarian strategies as a way to boost sales and build relationships. Sales professionals and recruiters who usually operate from a database or a leads list can take the opposite approach by actually determining which prospects on the list want to hear from them about future jobs or offers—by asking permission to keep in touch. A smart move, since not everyone is potentially your customer.

Seth Godin introduced the power and importance of asking permission in marketing and selling in his 1999 best seller, *Permission Marketing*. Seth's work and concept of "Permission Marketing" has only increased in importance as the market control has shifted from the salesperson—or company—to the consumer. The salesperson who understands this and learns to ask permission not only wins the hearts of potential clients but also has the ability to remain relevant, stay in sync with the market, and avoid interrupting people.

By seeking permission to keep in touch with potential customers, sales professionals in the medical industry can adopt the contrarian approach and do the following:

- Save time by calling only on the physicians interested in making a change—instead of wasting time and money by calling retired doctors or physicians who don't match the job qualifications.
- Build trust and credibility with potential clients by respecting their desire to stay on the list—rather than burning bridges by calling doctors who don't want solicitations about jobs.
- Make relevant and timely offers, knowing which physicians are ready to make a change and what conditions are needed for them to do so—rather than pitching jobs that are not a fit.
- Generate referrals to new doctors by building relationships with a network of physicians who are happy to recommend you—instead of creating enemies by offending influential members of your target market who have the ability to damage your reputation.

With the permission to follow up, sales professionals can then ask those physicians exactly what types of practice opportunities they are interested in pursuing. Knowing exactly what potential clients are wanting, sales professionals have more time to meet new potential prospects and grow their pipeline—rather than wasting energy and attempting to coerce a physician to consider a practice opportunity that doesn't fit.

After gaining permission, sales professionals can also learn to keep in touch by offering valuable and relevant information as a strategy to build trust and credibility, generate referrals, and open the door for potential sales. As the Ketchum research study suggests, potential clients are much more willing to listen to you and are interested in hearing more if you can find a way to be relevant.

All too often, sales professionals seem to think that relevance and keep-in-touch efforts equate to contacting potential clients repeatedly and consistently in hopes of closing the sale. Like the actor in the Verizon cell phone commercial who continuously asks the caller on the other end of his phone, "Can you hear me now? What about now?" uncertain of whether his message is getting through, salespeople who persistently ask closing questions at the end of each month are only pressuring their customers and destroying trust and credibility, not to mention losing sales.

This is not the contrarian way.

Instead of constantly trying to close the sale, companies can adopt a valuable keep-in-touch strategy that provides timely and meaningful information designed to help their potential customers find solutions to their problems.

Consider for a moment the e-mail lists you subscribe to and look forward to receiving. That will give you a sense of what you might want to use for your own keep-in-touch strategy. For medical sales professionals, this could take the form of a monthly article highlighting newsworthy events and trends in the medical industry that affect their prospects. Or it could be a weekly conference call designed to keep doctors apprised of the job opportunities by specialty and by region of the country. By offering relevant content, sales professionals have an opportunity to build a long-term relationship with their clients—something that you have an opportunity to do as well. The contrarian approach to keeping in touch not only means that the physician on the other end of the phone or e-mail has given you permission to keep in touch but that she gains value every time she hears from you. Which means that she thinks of you when she is ready to buy—all because you showed interest in her, took time to listen, and took steps to earn her trust. Instead of a single sale, the sales professional using the contrarian approach has a client for life, a client who refers 10 colleagues and who becomes a raving fan, telling everyone about her positive experiences with you.

Bull's-Eye

Royal Canin Canada, a pet food company, understands the power of the contrarian approach to sales.

In a MarketingProfs.com case study, "How a Pet Food Company Is Building a Loyal Customer Base via Highly Targeted Emails," writer Jennifer Nastu chronicles the success Royal Canin experienced as a result of implementing a particular contrarian strategy. The company adopted the strategy as a way to increase sales for its customized, breed-specific pet food sold in specialty stores. Royal Canin knew it had to distinguish itself from the hundreds of other pet food options available to its potential customers. The company also had to demonstrate why pet owners would want to pay a premium for the benefits that come from a food specially formulated for their dog's breed. The company understood that it would take doing something opposite of the conventional selling methods in order to win the business and the trust of the pet owners.

Instead of trying to convince customers to pay more for a pet food that they didn't know about, Royal Canin set out to earn the role of trusted advisor among its potential clients. By implementing "Pet First," a content-rich e-mail program, the company was able to build trust and credibility with potential clients over time. "Pet First," however, is not your average e-mail newsletter. In building relationships with potential customers, Royal Canin:

- Focused on bringing in loyal and active subscribers who would spread the word about the company—instead of assuming that all pet owners were ideal clients
- Created a highly targeted e-mail program specifically designed according to information collected about

the pet owner and the pet (including breed-specific tips and suggestions)—instead of sending out generic articles

- Allowed customers to tell the company when they were ready to buy—instead of asking for the sale again and again

The results are nothing less than remarkable. Eight months into the campaign, Royal Canin reported e-mail open rates of 95 percent and click-through rates of over 80 percent—incredible, given the average success rates. According to Bronto.com, average e-mail open rates as of March 2008 are 18.2 percent and e-mail click-through rates average around 4.3 percent. When asked about the results of the campaign, Royal Canin's Andrew Cannon is pleased. "With the core group of subscribers we've attracted," Cannon reports, "it's been extremely successful."

With e-mail click-through rates that are more than 20 times the average, Royal Canin's relevant, keep-in-touch campaign is successful indeed!

The Usual Suspects

"That's easier said than done," the veteran sales guy counters in thinking about the contrarian approach. It's understandable that sales managers and sales professionals in the trenches may initially resist adopting the Contrarian

Effect because they can't yet see how simple, easy, and profitable it can be to do so. For many seasoned sales professionals, the idea of staying relevant, timely, and current appears to be more work than they want to do right now.

In all fairness, why should they try the contrarian approach?

Many well-intentioned sales professionals argue that they continue to use the old tactics for one reason: They *believe* that they work. They also believe they have evidence demonstrating their effectiveness. This "evidence" can come from a variety of sources, such as training programs, sales books, sales seminars, first-hand experience, or stats reported by another company or another sales professional. These advocates also cite the typical tactics as "best practices," since other industry leaders or top companies report sales success in using the same techniques—a fact that cannot be verified unless you are a sales professional working for that organization.

While this evidence may appear to be strong and sound, it is often not directly linked to the results these sales managers want to achieve. In other words, the stats and evidence don't actually match up with the results created by the actual tactics themselves—a startling realization that Neil Rackham discovered as he was doing research for his book, *Spin Selling*.

Reasonable Doubt

When Rackham began the research, he was comfortable and familiar with the traditional tactics and theories on how to sell. He *believed* that his research would simply reinforce and validate the success of what he already knew. What the research actually uncovered, however, was something entirely different. As Rackham explains, "Research has an inconvenient way of coming up with evidence that the researchers sometimes wish they'd never found." In this case, Rackham actually discovered evidence *against* the successfulness of the classic tactics and support for contrarian methods:

When we started our investigations, our aim was to show that classic sales-training methods really worked and had a positive impact on sales success. It was only after we found a consistent failure of sales training to improve results in major sales that we began the long research road that led to the development of the methods described in this book. Before our research, I was happy to think of selling in the traditional terms that our findings now challenge.

In his study of closing techniques, the sales experts he consulted, which included writers, trainers, and experienced sales managers, believed that "closing . . . was the stage of the sale where the most crucial elements of success would be found." As the experts initially suggested, Rackham's research confirmed that closing techniques were indeed the most popular tactic, if not the most critical element of a successful sale.

Before he discovered research that proved otherwise, Rackham himself believed in the paramount importance of closing. In fact, he credited the "Alternative Close" as the reason for winning his first big piece of business. As a result of that success, one that he *felt* was due to his use of closing techniques, he "closed the hell out of everyone" during his first year of business, until his research proved that closing techniques were not the success factor he believed them to be:

---------------- ∾ ----------------

I now realize that I probably cost myself
and my company a lot of lost business during that
year. But at the time I was a totally convinced
hard closer. After all, my personal experience
showed that using an Alternative Close had
given me my first big piece of business.
I *knew* closing worked.

> I look back on my enthusiasm for closing with
> real embarrassment. From what I now know
> about success in the larger sale, I see closing
> techniques as both ineffective and dangerous.
> I've evidence that they lose much more
> business than they gain.

Instead of seeing a correlation between closing techniques and more sales, an association that many sales managers and trainers believed to be true at the time, Rackham repeatedly found closing to be negatively related to sales success and to be linked to lost sales.

As a result of his own experience, as well as his research that included observing more than 35,000 sales transactions, analyzing more than 116 factors that influence sales success, and studying effective selling in more than 27 countries over a 10-year period, Rackham drew two very important conclusions:

1. Attributing his sales success to the use of closing questions proved not to be true. As a result, he changed his belief surrounding the use of closing questions.
2. Closing questions, the most popular typical tactic, cause much more harm than good for the major sale.

Based on his research and his findings, Rackham abandoned his belief in the effectiveness of closing techniques.

Groundhog Day

Unlike Rackham, many sales professionals see glimpses of the market shift and specific evidence that the typical tactics no longer work and yet *still* choose to hold onto their beliefs in the traditional way of selling.

For example, many sales professionals still maintain a belief in traditional strategies like cold calling in order to prospect and connect with new leads and potential clients. While they may concede that cold calling might not work with every prospect, they believe it can be used on the next potential client with seemingly positive results. They may believe if they get enough prospects into their sales funnel, they are certain to get a few sales. In short, they perceive their work as a numbers game. "Sure, not everyone will buy," they admit, "but enough customers will buy to help me make my sales quotas." At least, that's the way they interpret their reality and their results.

Dan, a freelance photographer who sells his stock photography to magazines and other publications, feels that way.

After making a few attempts at communicating with clients in a more targeted and customized way, he gave up and went back to the usual approach. In fact, Dan has reverted back to mass marketing and doesn't bother to do anything other than send out generic e-mails to a mailing list he purchased. He defends his decision in a comment he made in response to Chris Anderson's October 2007 blog post (Anderson is editor in chief of *Wired* magazine and author of *The Long Tail*), which criticized the practice of sending unsolicited and irrelevant e-mails:

> Over the years, I have tried calling many of my intended targets but, when your market is magazine and book publishers all over the world and you have 7 to 10000 [sic] potential targets this can get expensive and impossibly time consuming. As well, the vast majority of creative buyers don't even bother returning your phone call. I've tried individual emails, which get an even lower response. So, I started sending out stock list updates via a mass emailing and the response has been nothing short of phenomenal. Yes, I do get requests to be taken off the list and there is a clear "unsubscribe" link at the bottom of every email but, only about 3% use it. I've also had potential buyers call me, tell me my work is great, ask to be taken off the list and put on the postcard only list. Others have called after receiving a promotional card and requested email only. The bottom line is, as a single entity operating a creative business, marketing to potential buyers is necessary, time consuming, expensive and difficult to do on an individual basis. As well, when the "broad brush" (okay, I'll call it spam) approach works as well as it does for me, it makes sense to keep doing it.

In his experience, the "personalized, nontypical approach" appeared to yield fewer results and cost him time and money, because he expected instantaneous results and because he was cold calling instead of contacting warm leads. And if that was the case, there's a very good chance he didn't give the new way sufficient time to work for him. He goes on to justify his decision to employ the conventional strategies, which he admits are spam, given his schedule and the demands he faces as a traveling photographer:

> I spent $10,000 this year on lists, email software, promotional cards etc. to promote my business and my work. You're on a list of people who buy creative work that is sold to photographers every day. If you don't really buy photography, why not just hit the unsubscribe button? Why give out your email? I get about 150 emails a day and travel 200+ days a year which makes it very difficult to get back to everyone after sorting through the spam I get but, it's an unfortunate part of the business and I unsubscribe to stuff that does not appeal to me.

In Dan's world, the apparent benefits of using a traditional tactic (buying a list and sending unsolicited e-mails to the people on that list) seem to be many, because he doesn't have other prospects giving him valuable feedback regarding the negative consequences of his actions and because he appears to be more interested in the immediate sale rather than building long-term relationships that result in repeat business. From Dan's perspective, he can spend more time on his photography and avoid the headache of customizing his direct outreach or devising new and different ways to reach his potential clients—strategies that may be far more effective and less costly than what he is doing now. But he continues to use the conventional way, even though he is doing something that will prompt prospects to block his e-mails and even though he received a public reprimand from a well-respected author and thought leader for doing so.

Tim Johnson feels the same way. Before adopting one of the oldest sales tactics in the book, Tim tried a variety of strategies, both traditional and contrarian, in order to reach prospects and to convert leads to sales. As a broker in the legal funding industry, his goal is simple: to connect with plaintiffs and attorneys. In launching his business, he invested heavily in direct mail campaigns and advertising. On the advice of a colleague in his industry, he networked with attorneys and paralegals in his target market. He even dabbled in some Internet-based strategies. Unfortunately, he felt that none of the strategies produced the results that he wanted. Like Dan, he didn't allow adequate time to test those customized strategies.

Nevertheless, he made a decision to adopt a few of the old-school selling strategies. Tim maintained he saw growth in his business when he implemented cold calling and walk-in visits to law firms as the two primary strategies in his sales process. He reported that he was able to produce more results with a list of law firms, a phone, a car, and 10 minutes to drop in on a law firm. By adopting cold calling and walk-in visits, he claims he was able to increase his sales, connect with more prospects, and reduce his overall costs.

Both Dan and Tim believe they *know* their industries. Based on Tim's own beliefs (but not necessarily statistics) and experiences with clients and law firms, he assumes that there's a very high probability that the law firm he visits today could use his services or refer him to its clients. So, while his colleagues are busy using direct mail or advertising, Tim spends his time going door to door because he believes it's the best way for him to meet clients and referral partners. Like Dan, Tim may not be hearing any negative feedback to the contrary, which reinforces his belief in the effectiveness of the tactics.

Additionally, both Dan and Tim *believe* they have tested and tried more personalized strategies and attempted to use something other than just the old-school methods. As a result of that "test," they maintain the belief that they close more sales using the tried-and-true sales tactics and system, which is unfortunate. Dan and Tim probably did what many sales professionals often do in trying to do the opposite. They may have done a little bit of research on potential target markets here and a little bit of warm calling there. Or they may have started a keep-in-touch strategy, such as a newsletter, for a few weeks or a month, expecting to see immediate results. They may have made a relevant offer to a handful of people, and when the sale didn't close immediately, they ditched them and returned to the old way. In the same way that its unrealistic for you to expect to lose 15 pounds or get in shape after a few trips to the gym, sales professionals rarely give the contrarian approach adequate time to generate potential clients and produce sales.

Is it possible that Dan and Tim are actually settling for less than the best by holding on to strategies that don't actually generate the results they seek?

The Little Engine That Could

Author and spiritual writer Thomas Merton believes that "the biggest human temptation is to settle for too little." By clinging to the old ways, ways that don't work now that their prospects are running the show, sales professionals like Dan and Tim will achieve less than they could if they adopted the contrarian approach.

For starters, Dan and Tim can begin by gaining permission to keep in touch with potential clients and referral sources so they can build relationships instead of constantly searching for new prospects every time they need to make a sale. They have a great opportunity to craft a follow-up strategy that allows them to offer value—free resources, articles, tips—in order to build trust and credibility with potential clients and to remain relevant and in sync with their target markets. In doing so, they save hours and hours of time in cold-calling people and interrupting them, many of whom will never buy from them. But there's even more.

By adopting two contrarian strategies, Dan and Tim can reach far more qualified prospects in much less time:

1. *Identify and target specific groups of individuals, rather than the mass market.*

As part of their international survey, Ketchum describes the new market reality as the "public of one," a concept that highlights the importance of communicating with and targeting individuals and distinct groups of individuals, rather than the faceless many. Instead of using the typical tactics to broadcast a one-way message to the masses and to target everyone with a pulse and a checkbook, Dan and Tim can benefit greatly by spending a small amount of time clarifying the following points:

- What are the qualities of the people with whom they do their best work?
- What are the specific demographics of the distinct group of people they want to reach?

If you ask average customers whom they prefer to do business with, they will tell you that they like to buy from those that they "know, like, and trust." Naturally. After all, why would a potential customer want to buy from someone they don't know, don't necessarily like, and definitely don't trust?

If customers respond best to the sales professionals who match these criteria, it's only logical that the customer-salesperson affinity works both ways. Yet many sales professionals expect to or feel pressured to work with high-maintenance, demanding, or unpleasant customers because they feel they have to have the sale. Choosing to do business with your less-than-ideal clients comes with a price—a high price. The wrong customers cost you time, money, and energy and zap your motivation and drive needed to identify and communicate with the right customers—a major buzzkill that can tank your productivity.

There's an easy solution for this. It's called the "Red Velvet Rope Policy," a concept coined by Michael in his best seller, *Book Yourself Solid*.

By identifying the qualities and traits of the people with whom you do your best work, you are giving yourself an incredible advantage over the salesperson sitting next to you, struggling to serve a stable of hard-to-please prospects and customers. When you work with the clients who embody the personality traits and interests that inspire you to do your best work, you automatically save time and energy and earn more money as a result. Why? Because working with the clients you naturally resonate with is easy and effortless, allowing you more time to find more clients like them and make sales in less time.

Take a moment and think about the qualities of your best clients, the ones you want more of. Are they intelligent, positive, quick learners? Are they creative, artistic, and open to new ideas? Think about the people you most like to be around, those who inspire you and give you the most energy. These are the people with whom you do your best work, the ones who are allowed past your Red Velvet Rope. Applying the test also means that the customers who want services you can't or don't want to provide, who have unreasonable expectations, or who suck the life out of you are less-than-ideal clients for you, even though they might be great clients for someone else.

In addition to establishing a Red Velvet Rope to filter out the less-than-desirable prospects, Dan and Tim can more effectively connect with ideal prospects by getting a clear picture of their target markets, the distinct group of individuals most likely to benefit from their products and services. This cannot happen when you buy a leads lists and send out broadcast e-mails or cold-call every business that belongs to an industry category.

Both Dan and Tim can do themselves a favor by outlining exactly what groups they are intending to reach. For Dan, is it magazines? Newspapers? From there, Dan can drill down to identify the specific types of magazines and publications that most need his services and communicate with them in a way that speaks to their needs. Since the needs and desires of end users of a business magazine like *Wired* are completely different from those of a magazine like *Home and Garden,* Dan can save enormous amounts of time and money by:

- Isolating and defining the specific subgroups and clusters of publications that are most likely to purchase his photography based on past experiences and on their actual needs and desires, rather than on his perception of what they want or need
- Investigating how to reach the key decision makers of these subgroups in order to build trust and credibility with them over time
- Determining the best ways to communicate with these distinct groups—whether it be via e-mail, phone, newsletter, or all of these—so that he can provide relevant and timely content as part of his follow-up strategy

In following these strategies, Dan may determine that he is targeting three or four different and unique subgroups, which is fine as long as he remembers to communicate with each group as a unique entity. A blanket communication to all of those groups won't do the trick.

Once Dan identifies the detailed demographics of his target market, he can further identify the ideal clients, the ones who pass the Red Velvet Rope test, who are part of the larger target market. In doing so, he can identify the prospects who want to hear from him and want to receive communication from him, even if they are not ready to buy.

2. *Collaborate with strategic partners who share the same target market.*

A second contrarian strategy that both Dan and Tim can immediately implement is to find ways to collaborate and work with others who serve the same target market. Instead of cold calling, what if Tim found strategic partners and other service professionals who already work with his target market? By forming relationships with them and leveraging their efforts, he has a faster and more efficient way to meet and build relationships with potential clients. Additionally, he can get warm introductions and meet far more of them in less time. In turn, the strategic partner benefits by meeting the potential clients who are a part of Tim's permission-based prospect group. This strategy allows both Tim and his collaboration partner to profit from the work of two people rather than from their individual efforts. Here's a specific example of how Tim can collaborate and win.

Suppose Tim meets a business consultant who also works with family law firms having no more than 10 attorneys. Together they can:

- Host business receptions and events that allow the family law attorneys to grow their own networks and that connect them with strategic partners they need to know, such as accountants and high-level financial advisors
- Cut down on the time it takes to build trust and credibility with prospects by introducing in their monthly newsletter or blog post their strategic partner as a recommended resource
- Understand how to best refer business to one another, ensuring that they can give each other high-quality referrals
- Introduce each other to additional strategic partners and centers of influence in their network

On his own, Tim is able to meet only a handful of attorneys, if that.

In collaborating with strategic partners, Tim can quickly meet all of the top attorneys in his city and grow his network by several hundred people overnight. And not just strangers, but prospects and strategic partners who already know and like Tim because he was referred to them by someone they already know, like, and trust. This means more sales in less time, but without alienating prospects or pressuring potential customers to buy when they are not ready.

Like Dan and Tim, you have an opportunity to shift gears and head in the opposite direction. You can access the knowledge and apply the strategies you need to thrive in today's customer-driven market. You can quickly and easily begin to implement the contrarian strategies, starting today, by:

- Choosing to work with your ideal clients—the ones with whom you do your best work (Red Velvet Rope Policy)
- Clarifying the distinct groups of individuals that comprise your target market (the "public of one")
- Collaborating with strategic partners and other business professionals who serve the same target market in order to reach more prospects with less effort
- Asking for permission to keep in touch with potential prospects and clients
- Creating a relevant and value-based follow-up process that builds trust and credibility

Your prospects and clients will thank you for it.

Center of the Universe

*Typical Tactics Are Focused
on the Wrong Person*

The Butcher, the Baker, the Candlestick Maker

In 1776, Scottish economist Adam Smith wrote his treatise, *An Inquiry into the Nature and Causes of the Wealth of Nations.* Smith's treatise is considered one of the first contemporary works in the field of economics.

In *Wealth of Nations,* Smith discusses the importance of the pursuit of self-interest as a critical element in the foundation of free market economics. Specifically, he explains that:

It is not from the benevolence of the butcher, the brewer, or the baker that we expect our dinner, but from their regard to their own self-interest. We address ourselves, not to their humanity but to their self-love, and never talk to them of our own necessities but of their advantages.

Said another way, it is our self-interest that drives us to serve others and to act, whether that means cooking a meal, driving someone to the airport, taking care of our children, saying a kind word, giving a referral, or making a sale. According to Smith, self-interest is essential to the flow of goods and services.

But it's more than just an economic force. Self-interest is essential to our survival as humans.

The importance of self-interest in prompting people to act, both you and your customers, is evidenced by the popular, modern-day acronym WIIFM. It's another way of asking the question, "What's in it for me?" Understanding this concept saves us from reading Smith's *Wealth of Nations,* a work that's obviously not leisure reading for a Sunday afternoon.

Here's the bottom line. Self-interest is just about as important as eating and drinking. It's the driving force that compels us to act. It's the motivator that prompts potential clients to buy from you instead of sitting at home in front of the TV. It's also the catalyst that prompts a customer to buy from you rather than from your competitor. But self-interest operates on both sides of the equation. While WIIFM is a phrase often used to remind sales professionals to focus on their customers' needs and desires, it applies to the salesperson as well. After all, why in the world would you willingly choose a job that subjects you to constant rejection and blows to the ego? C'mon. No one loves selling that much. As with your customer, self-interest drives you to continue to prospect and search for that ideal customer.

Which creates a bit of a conundrum. How can you, Mr. Sales Ace, operate out of your own self-interest at the same time that your customer is operating out of her own self-interest? While it's certainly possible for your customer's self-interest to be in harmony with your own, it's not probable. Most often, the customer has different needs and motivations, ones that often clash with your own self-interest.

It's at that moment when self-interest often morphs into selfishness on the part of the sales professional. As Swiss philosopher Henri Frederic Amiel explains, "Self-interest is but the survival of the animal in us. Humanity only begins for man with self-surrender."

There's nothing wrong with the salesperson's acting out of self-interest. The problem begins when self-interest morphs into selfishness. Sales professionals often put their own needs and desires ahead of those of their customers, partly because the traditional sales process focuses on the selling process rather than the buying process. As a result, sales professionals cannot focus on the needs and desires of their customers or pay attention to their customer's buying process. When they use the typical tactics, many sales professionals struggle, and usually fail, to respect the customer's timing and speed. That effect is amplified with a sales professional who is overtly more concerned with selling than with doing what's right for the customer.

This often creates problems. Just ask Augustus, Violet, Veruca, and Mike.

Oompa, Loompa, Doopity Dee

In the movie *Willy Wonka and the Chocolate Factory,* selfish behavior is not only subject to quirky and unusual punishments, but it is the theme of the impromptu songs spontaneously performed by the Oompa Loompas, the pint-sized factory workers who help Mr. Wonka make the chocolate bars, confections, and other sugary delights.

Based on the novel by Roald Dahl, the movie tells the story of Mr. Willy Wonka, a reclusive and eccentric chocolate factory owner who decides to open his factory to the five lucky winners of a Golden Ticket. In order to win the highly sought-after ticket, children all over the world rush to candy stores, buying up as many Wonka bars as they can, hoping that their Wonka bar is one of the five special bars containing the Golden Ticket.

Four of the five tickets are claimed almost immediately. These four winners, Augustus Gloop, Violet Beauregarde, Veruca Salt, and Mike Teevee, are spoiled and bratty kids whose parents spare no expense in order for them to discover a Golden Ticket. Then there's Charlie, a poor child with enough money to purchase two Wonka bars and the lucky winner of the last ticket. In contrast to the others, Charlie is generous, kind, and sensitive, traits that do not go unnoticed by Mr. Wonka when the children begin their tour of the chocolate factory.

Unaware of Mr. Wonka's real motivations for opening up his factory, the children act without pretense and without an attempt to impress or influence Willy Wonka's perceptions of them. Too bad that Augustus, Violet, Veruca, and Mike do not realize Mr. Wonka's intention is to choose a successor to run his factory from the group of five who won a Golden Ticket. If they had known, they might have tempered their selfish behavior.

All the children except Charlie behave in a selfish fashion, grabbing as much candy as they can and breaking the rules of the factory. Their self-serving behaviors result in some peculiar and unusual punishments. Gluttonous Augustus Gloop is sucked into the chocolate river pipes after disregarding the warnings not to drink from the river. As Augustus disappears into the river, the Oompa Loompas, clearly unimpressed with him, spontaneously break out in song and denigrate him for his selfish behavior.

As for the other children, Violet Beauregarde is turned into a giant blueberry after defiantly grabbing the experimental chewing gum. Veruca Salt takes a trip down the garbage chute as a result of her greedy behavior. And Mike Teevee becomes a tiny television set after repeatedly asking his dad if he can buy certain parts of the factory.

In the end, Charlie is the only child left. Mr. Wonka gives him the keys to the factory as a result of his selfless attitude and kind behavior.

In the movie, Charlie is a contrarian of sorts. Unlike the other children, he puts the needs of elderly grandparents ahead of his own. He works to put food on the table and doesn't demand his own way as the other children do. He is giving, generous, and kind to all those around him. Although Charlie's attitude and actions don't initially seem to benefit him, Charlie ends up winning big in the end, demonstrating that it pays to take the "road less traveled."

Additionally, Charlie demonstrates that it's not just about how you behave, but it's also about who you are as a person. Choosing the contrarian way is not only about adopting new strategies, new communication techniques, and new actions that serve the best interests of the customer, but also about having the right attitude and the right intentions. Like Charlie, you can decide right now to do what's best for your customers and to put their needs ahead of your own. No new strategies needed for that. You can choose to offer information and value without expecting or demanding anything in return. You can choose to respect the timing and pace of sale that works for the customer instead of what you need or prefer.

Easier Is Not Always Better

Unfortunately, many sales professionals do not realize that their self-interest has morphed into selfish attitudes and self-serving behavior.

For example, Gary Dunn continues to send Elizabeth monthly e-mails asking her to renew her subscription to his publication, *The Caretaker Gazette*, which she let lapse over five years ago. Perhaps he chooses the typical tactics because it's easier for him.

No offense to Gary, but there's a reason Elizabeth let her subscription lapse. *The Caretaker Gazette* is a great little publication—but only if you are in need of temporary housing or want to live in another part of the country while house-sitting for someone else. Because Gary continues to use typical tactics in hopes of capturing her business, he doesn't know that:

- His renewal e-mails feel outdated and irrelevant, since Elizabeth's needs and circumstances are vastly different from when she initially subscribed to his publication. Because his offer is not relevant, there's no chance she will renew right now and very little chance she will renew later.

- His offer seems more about him, the salesperson, than about Elizabeth. Each month, the e-mail subject line reads, "Please renew your subscription to *The Caretaker Gazette*." Perhaps she missed the point, but the offer appears to be all about what he stands to gain and not at all about the benefits she is missing, such as discounts, special articles, or bonus offers, if she doesn't renew.

Elizabeth doesn't know Gary personally, but she feels inclined to give him the benefit of the doubt here. He may not be aware of the fact that she perceives his e-mails as self-serving—although she would be happy to give him that feedback if he asked—mainly because he does not point out any benefits or any reasons she should renew her subscription other than the fact that it will help him, although he may not intend to promote his needs (to generate more income through renewals) over hers.

But the fact remains that it's hard to see the e-mails as anything more than a pitch crafted to help him meet his goals. He chooses the easiest and most cost-effective way for him, the salesperson, instead of the way it would be best for her, the customer. Whether he intends it or not, his sales offer is all about him and not at all about her.

Your customers and prospects are quite observant and aware of self-serving offers like that. As a result, they resist and avoid many attempts from sales professionals to contact them.

Jill Konrath, author of *Selling to Big Companies,* best describes this resistance in her poem titled "The Buyer's Lament."

> Don't waste my time, please go away.
> I will not talk with you today.
> You call me up, you want to sell.
> But all you do is tell, tell, tell.
> I do not want to hear your spiel.
> I will not play let's make a deal.

> So listen up, take my advice.
> Discover how you can entice.

This first section echoes the "me-me-me" attitude that many customers can sense, or overtly observe, in their interactions with those who employ the typical tactics.

In the second half of the poem, the "buyer" goes on to share the secrets of how to best communicate with her, get a foot in the door, and win her sale if the salesperson can only shift his focus away from himself and onto the customer:

> If you aspire to earn my trust,
> Research is an absolute must.
> Know my goals, the issues I face.
> Use this to build your business case.
> What have you done for firms like mine?
> How have you helped their bottom line?
> Can you cut my costs or help me grow?
> Now that's the info I want to know.
> If you can help me solve my plight,
> I'm wide open to fresh insight.
> I need to find new perspectives
> So I can reach my objectives.
> Want me to remember your name?
> Launch an account entry campaign.
> Ten contacts is what it may take,

When there's so much business at stake.
Just think of this next time you phone
And you'll get past my no-entry zone.
Once you get your foot in the door,
I guarantee you'll sell lots more!

In a lighthearted way, the poem pokes fun at the unfortunate reality of selling that is more common than most of us would like to admit—one that tends to be focused on the salesperson rather than on the customer, a world in which self-serving salespeople:

- Show the customer the benefits they can provide—instead of listening for and understanding the customer's needs and desires
- Tell the customer about their services—ones that may not be relevant or valuable to the prospect
- Sell their services long before they've established the trust and credibility needed to make the sale
- Talk, talk, talk—instead of listening
- Close—too early and too often
- Assume they can follow up—instead of asking whether it's okay to call the prospect again

Sales professionals who use the typical tactics often get caught up in a game of show-and-tell. Unlike the game in which children get to show a favorite toy and tell the whole class about it, your prospects are no longer willing participants in the one-sided game.

It's All Fun and Games Until . . .

Chris Anderson experienced the "me first" attitude directly and decided to let the world know about it. In a controversial blog post in October 2007, the *Wired* magazine editor in chief voiced his frustration over the amount of unsolicited press releases he had received in the previous month.

In a post titled, "Sorry PR People: You're Blocked," he not only questioned the validity and the effectiveness of the blanket press release, but publicly censured a list of around 300 PR people for not bothering to confirm whether he indeed wanted them to clamor for his attention in the way that they did.

He explained:

> So fair warning: I only want two kinds of email: those from people I know, and those from people who have taken the time to find out what I'm interested in and composed a note meant to appeal to that (I love those emails; indeed, that's why my email address is public).
>
> Everything else gets banned on first abuse. The following is just the last month's list of people and companies who have been added to my Outlook blocked list. All of them have sent me something inappropriate at some point in the past 30 days. Many of them sent press releases; others just added me to a distribution list without

> asking. If their address gets harvested by spammers by being published here, so be it—turnabout is fair play.
>
> There is no getting off this list. If you're on it and have something appropriate to say to me, use a different email address.

He went on to cite individually the e-mail address of each PR person who had violated his wishes and spammed him with their unspecific and irrelevant pitch.

Harsh? Some say yes (and they let him know that by posting their comments on his post). Understandable? Absolutely. Criticized as a rant by some and lauded as a long-overdue moment of truth by others, Chris's post supports the argument that what used to be effective in reaching potential customers may actually serve to repel them and cause them to resist you.

Whether or not you agree with Chris's public announcement, here's the point. He is no longer willing or open to any offer or pitch from those salespeople, regardless of how relevant or timely it may be. And because many of the typical sales tactics are used without permission from the prospect or potential customer, customers frequently react by ignoring, deleting, or turning a deaf ear to what's actually being offered.

Customer Bill of Rights

Rather than convincing prospects to play a game of show-and-tell or adjust to your preference for the traditional sales process, you can adopt the contrarian approach. Simply ask your prospects questions about how they would like to be treated, how they want to be communicated with, and whether they want to hear from you again. As with the narrator in Jill Konrath's poem, today's prospects demand that you:

- Listen to them and understand their needs and desires
- Tell the truth and be radically transparent
- Respect them and their ability to buy from anyone, anytime
- Honor their timetable and their buying schedule
- Allow them to buy in the way that works for them
- Be authentic and sincere
- Ask permission to keep in touch
- Keep your word and honor your commitments
- Treat them as intelligent people capable of making a good decision

Can't Buy Me Love

This reality is not only a way of being that you can adopt today, but it's something you can demonstrate to potential clients and prospects to build trust and credibility quickly. In his best-selling book *Love Is the Killer App,* Tim Sanders outlines the importance—and the payoff—of sharing your intangibles with your customers and referral partners. Tim's strategy is easy to implement, takes almost no time at all, and costs you nothing. Here's how it works.

Michael meets a potential client at a conference or through a friend. After a brief chat, Michael shares his knowledge in the form of a book recommendation or resource that is most relevant to what he knows about that person so far. Immediately, Michael has done two things: He has provided immediate value to that prospect, and he has established enough rapport and trust for that prospect to want Michael to keep in touch with him. By taking a few seconds to share his intangibles, Michael now has permission to follow up, which is the most important step in setting the stage for a long-term relationship.

Sharing your intangibles is also a key strategy to use as part of the sales cycle. All too often, sales professionals fall into the trap of asking for the sale too often and too early. Rather than forcing the sale, take the contrarian approach and follow up with relevant and timely information for your potential prospects, which includes sharing your network.

Elizabeth can simultaneously build trust and credibility and follow up with prospects by sharing her network, a strategy that takes less than two minutes and doesn't cost a dime. In other words, she can introduce prospects to someone in her circle of influence who can offer immediate value to those prospects in some way. As a result, she stays "top of mind" with her prospects, who will not only appreciate the introduction but will remember her when they are ready to buy.

After all, you can't buy attention. You have to earn it.

By sharing your knowledge, your network, and your compassion—honesty, sincerity, and genuine concern for your prospects—you win the hearts of potential clients and earn their attention and respect. Which translates into not only short-term sales but repeat sales and referrals.

Membership Has Its Privileges

Jim Sinegal, founder and CEO of Costco Wholesale, understands the importance of sharing your intangibles. By taking the contrarian approach, he enjoys the benefits that come from over 45 million loyal members who regularly shop in 531 Costco stores across the United States and in eight countries around the world.

Sinegal's approach is simple yet brilliant: Take care of your customers, and take care of your employees. After all, well-treated employees are happier and will want to take better care of your customers.

Because Costco is a place where customers feel respected and know that they come first, *they pay for the privilege to shop there,* happily spending a minimum of $50 in annual membership fees. According to customer Jose Davila, Costco "is the best place in the world. It's like going to church on Sunday. You can't get anything better than this. This is a religious experience."

That's just one example of how customers feel about Costco. They express their good feelings for the retail leader by spending lots and lots of money there. In a 2006 article, *20/20* correspondents Alan B. Goldberg and Bill Ritter confirm that customers don't just express loyalty with nice testimonials. Attorney Ray Dinari spends over $25,000 per year at Costco, buying everything from clothing to food to electronics—everything except his business suits. He buys those at the Armani store. Now *that's* repeat business.

By treating customers well, Sinegal can generate thousands of dollars in sales per customer by doing the opposite— putting the customer ahead of profits or the needs of the company.

With more than $60 billion in annual sales, Costco focuses on pleasing its customers and creating an environment that allows its customers to buy—without spending a dime on advertising or PR. Sinegal believes that approach is the right way to build a business:

───────────── ∾ ─────────────

Our code of ethics says we have to obey the law. We have to take care of our customers, take care of our people. And if we do those things, we think that we'll reward our shareholders.

According to Goldberg and Ritter, the only people that wonder about Sinegal's unconventional practices are Wall Street analysts. They see opportunities for Costco to earn even more profits and grow its sales, but at the expense of employee wages. To increase sales, analysts recommend that Sinegal cut the average wage of $17 an hour down to something akin to what Wal-Mart pays its employees.

Rather than slashing employee wages or taking away programs that build customer loyalty, Sinegal continues to take the contrarian approach, convinced it will continue to pay big dividends in the long run. As he explains:

Wall Street is in the business of making money between now and next Tuesday. We're in the business of building an organization and an institution that we hope will be here 50 years from now. And paying good wages and keeping your people working with you is very good business.

With a higher sales volume than Sam's Club, Costco's main competitor, Sinegal has data and evidence that the contrarian approach is not only the right way to go, but the best way to generate long-term profits.

Good business indeed.

Bless Your Heart, You Pathetic, Spineless Jellyfish

Even with contrarian role models like Sinegal and Costco, sales professionals continue to use the traditional sales approach, thinking they won't seem self-serving to the customers on the other side of the table.

"With the right motivation and the right approach, I can use the typical tactics successfully," retorts the sales guy, loyal to the old strategies. For sales professionals like him, it appears possible to use them without coming across as a selfish pig.

C'mon now. Is it *really* possible to look at sales from a buyer's perspective if you are using the traditional sales approach and traditional tactics?

That argument is not unlike the ongoing debate about the meaning of a particular Southern phrase.

If you ask any Alabama or Georgia resident what "Bless your heart" really means, you're likely to get conflicting answers and differing opinions. If you have never used this phrase before or been in conversation with someone who has, then you may not see what all the fuss is about.

Clearly, the debate is not over the greater philosophical meaning inherent in such a simple statement. Rather, the debate is over whether "Bless her heart" is an endearing compliment or an underhanded insult. So that you get an idea of how this works, here are some examples:

Example: Mary just lost her job due to layoffs, bless her heart.

Meaning: Too bad for Mary, since she is a sharp gal and hard worker.

Example: Bill just won Salesman of the Year, bless his heart!

Meaning: Congratulations to Bill! He's a very talented guy.

Example: Sales is not the best profession for Tim, bless his heart.

Meaning: Tim is not the sharpest tool in the shed. He's going to lose his shirt if he doesn't wise up and change careers.

Example: That hairstyle doesn't fit her, bless her heart.

Meaning: Her stylist obviously failed to tell her that haircut is all wrong for her face and doesn't look professional. I feel bad for her.

You get the point. Depending upon the tone, inflection, or intention of the person speaking, "Bless your heart" can be a sincere compliment and indication of care and concern, or it can be a subtle criticism or a condescending remark disguised as a nice one. As the recipient, it's up to you to determine whether you're receiving a compliment or a slap in the face, bless your heart.

In the same way someone believes that you can use "Bless your heart" as either a sincere or a rude remark, the sales professionals in favor of the old way believe they have the power and control to determine how the typical tactics come across to their customers. For example, they may argue that they can use traditional sales strategies with the right motivation and with the right approach and successfully put the customer first. Those in favor of cold calling *believe* they can successfully use that tactic for the potential client's benefit, even though cold calling, by definition, means that such salespeople are interrupting them with unsolicited phone calls. They *feel* that closing tactics designed to speed up the sale can be highly effective if used in the right way and at the right time, even though this is nearly impossible, given the self-serving nature of the typical tactics.

Indecent Proposal

It's understandable that advocates of the typical tactics think this is possible. They have seen legendary sales trainers and sales professionals with a high level of mastery demonstrate these tactics at sales training events or workshops—and make it look easy. As a result of those experiences, they maintain the belief that they, too, can use them with the same precision and skill as the sales master they observed onstage.

This is an illusion. After all, *the traditional sales process and selling tactics were designed with the seller in mind—not the buyer.*

Like the skilled surgeon who can make do with outdated, crude surgical tools and still perform a surgical procedure successfully, the sales master can cold-call and use closing techniques without creating an absolute mess. In the same way that many less experienced surgeons would have an incredibly difficult time using the old tools to operate without butchering their patients, many sales professionals cannot help but destroy a perfectly good relationship and potential sale when they use the typical tactics. The traditional strategies and methods are not unlike blunt objects, unrefined tools that are not capable of doing much other than inflicting brute force on their recipients.

For this reason, many sales masters and experienced pros choose not to use the typical tactics any longer. While they can *technically* use them with skill, they have moved on to better, more up-to-date and more effective selling processes and selling methods. After all, why would you want to use crude and archaic strategies when there are many savvy, current ones at your disposal?

Sales expert Jill Konrath, author of *Selling to Big Companies* and one of the most well-respected and talented selling professionals in the industry, shares a story about what can happen when you rely on traditional sales tactics to get customers:

> I was so excited to be starting my sales career at Xerox. They were known for having the best sales training in their industry. Newly hired sales reps were expected to memorize their copier presentations word-for-word.
>
> Before we were allowed to make sales calls, we had to demonstrate this competence to our sales manager. Wanting to excel, I practiced my script over and over and over:
>
> "Mr. Prospect, for years Xerox has designed copiers to meet the needs of our customers. Our experience and success in the marketplace shows that regardless of specific needs there are four primary criteria customers use in selecting their copy machine . . . quality, reliability, versatility, and ease-of-operation."
>
> When I thought I was ready for prime time, I stood before my sales manager and gave my schpiel. When I invariably screwed it up, she'd tell me, "Keep working on it."
>
> One day I finally nailed it. My manager smiled and said, "Now you're ready. Go get 'em." I'll never forget the first time I gave the presentation to a real live prospect. When he came to our office for a demo, I was a bit nervous, but also relieved that I knew just what to say. I brought him over to our new copier, which was a perfect fit for his needs. He stood beside me as I began the demonstration. The memorized script was perfectly inscribed on my brain. I didn't forget one single word!

And, throughout my entire presentation I called him "Mr. Prospect." Worse yet, he never even corrected me or smiled. You can't believe how incredibly stupid I felt when I realized what I'd done.

It was at that moment in time that I realized sales was not about canned presentations or manipulative techniques. It was about focusing on your customer's specific needs, challenges, issues, or objectives.

Most sales greats and master sales professionals like Jill have let go of the rudimentary tools and techniques and moved on to the Contrarian Effect. Shouldn't you?

Coffee Is for Closers

Much to his detriment, Jim is a sales professional who still insists on using closing tactics, believing he can use them without butchering a potential sale. While a few of his customers may consider questions such as "Shall I wrap that up for you?" or "What additional questions can I answer so that you are ready to purchase XYZ service?" helpful, Michael did not.

As a potential customer attempting to purchase a customer relationship management system (CRM) from the well-known, nationally recognized company that employed Jim, Michael certainly found them to be off-putting and aggressive. Especially considering that Jim knew the conditions that had to be in place before Michael would purchase his CRM system.

Jim, the first salesman who contacted Michael about purchasing the system, appeared to want to help. Jim was responsive in answering Michael's questions and educating him about his product. While Michael felt that the system was one that could meet his needs, he needed to determine one thing before purchasing the CRM system. Michael stressed to Jim that Michael's programmer had to ensure that he could build a software application to integrate all of Michael's customer and client data between his online system and this new CRM system. Jim seemed to understand Michael's specific needs, since he extended the trial period for the software a number of times so that the Michael's programmer could access it in order to create the necessary software application to integrate Michael's existing database with Jim's CRM system.

Despite his seemingly helpful demeanor, it was clear that Jim was focused more on his commissions and his sales numbers than on Michael's needs as a customer. Jim's persistent calls and urgent e-mails reflected his focus on closing the sale on his own timetable and on furthering his own goals. In fact, he made no attempt to conceal the real motivation for his calls and e-mails. With each communication, he emphasized to Michael that it was the end of the month and he'd "really like to hit his numbers" and he's "hoping to make something happen before the end of the week or perhaps even the end of the day."

Again, he's a really nice fellow, but Michael is not buying this system from him. And he's certainly not buying it according to Jim's timetable so that Jim can make his numbers.

Managers often set up processes that are meant to incentivize salespeople. What these processes do instead is put pressure on salespeople to in turn put pressure on potential customers. What are the consequences of such a reality? A seemingly innocent and harmless cold call, unsolicited e-mail, or an attempt to close the sale early can inflict long-term damage and unintended consequences, whether the salesperson is simply focused on herself over the customer or whether she is feeling the pressure from the company to close sales. Either way, the tactics usually shut down sales instead of opening them.

Opening Doors and Opening Possibilities

Jim and his company can take the contrarian approach and do the opposite.

Instead of pressuring prospects to buy before they are ready, Jim can keep in touch with potential clients by offering them something of value. Something relevant that causes the prospect to want to keep in touch with him—and even welcome his calls—instead of screening him out. That something we call the "Always Have Something to Invite People To" offer.

Specifically, Jim and his company can set up and sponsor a free conference call or webinar series in which they educate potential and existing customers on the best ways to manage a sales pipeline, stay on top of communication with prospects, and manage the sales process—with specific examples of how their CRM system helps clients do that. Or Jim's company can sponsor a "best of business" series by bringing in business experts and authors to share strategies and tips for increasing sales and growing business.

With a value-rich free offering, Jim's company would be able to:

- Give something of immediate value and use to customers considering their services
- Build trust and credibility with both future and existing clients
- Keep in touch with prospects without constantly asking them to buy
- Reach far more prospects at once by leveraging the power of groups
- Offer the free call to strategic partners and businesses with the same target market so that those companies also have something of value to offer prospects

By hosting a regular call or webinar series, Jim and the sales team would always have a no-risk offer to extend to target clients, an offer that doesn't pressure customers to move faster than they want, which creates an interesting effect. In slowing down the sales cycle and giving something of value away without asking for anything in return, sales actually happen faster than they would with the typical tactics. Here's how.

In using the "Always Have Something to Invite People To" offer, Jim can create the environment in which the best and most qualified prospects will emerge and approach him. Rather than chasing down prospects, Jim can field calls and questions from customers who are ready to buy right now. No closing or coercion is needed to close these deals. Sales are easy when it's the right time for the customer. At the same time, he can build relationships with the potential clients who are not ready to buy yet by inviting them to his weekly or monthly events, ones with little risk and with no barrier to entry.

This is the primary strategy that Michael has used to grow his database to over 40,000 subscribers and potential clients. By hosting a free weekly call as part of his "Think Big Revolution," small business owners and service professionals can tune in each Monday at 12 P.M. Eastern time to learn about strategies and tools to help them increase their sales right away. Because the call has no strings attached, Michael can make this offer right away without damaging his reputation or without forcing a sale. For example, you can go to www.michaelport.com and join the revolution. It will help you think bigger about who you are and what you offer the world—without costing you anything.

As a result, Michael is able to connect with thousands more customers than if he were trying to pitch one of his high-dollar services. In doing so, Michael can easily:

- Increase the "know, like, and trust" factor by giving prospects an experience of what it's like to work with him
- Build trust and credibility much faster than he otherwise would—which have to be present in order for sales to happen
- Follow up with clients in a relevant and meaningful way by inviting them to the weekly call
- Speed up sales by giving frequent and consistent opportunities for prospects to experience his services without risk

A business software company, Softrax, more than doubled its sales after it implemented a free monthly "Always Have Something to Invite People To" offer.

Like Jim's company, Softrax sells a high-end software solution with a lengthy sales cycle. And like Jim, the Softrax sales professionals have a challenge: They need to build trust and credibility with potential clients, to follow up with prospects in a relevant and valuable way, and to speed up the sales cycle without negatively impacting the client.

Instead of calling and asking for the sale, Softrax positioned itself as a trusted advisor. By hosting the "Executive Webcast Series," a free monthly webinar in which a Softrax executive interviewed a government or industry expert, the company quickly became a valuable resource and place for executives to come learn about best practices and most helpful ways to manage their company revenue cycles. As a result of implementing this contrarian strategy, Softrax was able to:

- Connect with qualified and interested executives within its target market
- Build trust and credibility with 500 to 600 potential clients in a single webinar
- Speed up the sales cycle by offering relevant content
- Position itself as an industry expert, encouraging customers to buy

- Provide a free offering for its sales professionals to provide value to potential clients and strategic partners

Since instituting the webinar series, Softrax sales have gone from $12 million to over $27 million, thus creating a Contrarian Effect, one that attracts far more customers than if the company tried to push for the sale or promote the benefits of its product without any additional value. According to company director Stephen Foster, the webinar is "far and away one of our most effective vehicles" to increase sales. Foster is confident that adopting the contrarian approach was a smart decision:

We know we're doing it right. We continue to see phenomenal growth, and we hold our head high. There's a lot of integrity in how we market our products.

Jim and his company can do the same and reach far more prospects with less effort by using the "Always Have Something to Invite People To" strategy. It sure beats nagging customers—and wasting time—on those who are not ready to buy.

One-Night Stand

Typical Tactics Damage
Relationships and
Long-Term Potential

IF YOU ASK MICHAEL'S SON, Jake, whether he wants a piece of candy right now, he will instantly exclaim, "Now, Daddy, now!" We can sympathize with a toddler's or young child's lack of impulse control and inability to delay gratification. After all, how can you possibly fault a child for wanting a juicy morsel of sugary goodness when it is available right now? Children haven't been conditioned enough to act otherwise. Clearly, self-interest seems for all of us, regardless of age, a birthright. As it is with self-interest, the desire for instant gratification and immediate reward is instinctual to us as humans.

Somewhere along the path of development, however, we learn from our parents and teachers that seeking and even demanding immediate gratification is not usually beneficial. "Patience is a virtue," we are told. Also, if we delay the rewards, we can gain even more.

Want to lose weight? You've got to forgo eating sweets, cut back on carbs, and get up early so you can get to the gym before work.

Want to take that vacation? You've got to cut back on dining out, taking trips to the mall, and buying that new HDTV.

Adults, truth be told, are no different than Michael's son. We want the rewards, and we want them *now*!

Which is why game shows like *Deal or No Deal* and *Who Wants to Be a Millionaire?* are big hits. These reality shows play on the basic human desires for instant reward and gratification. They also tug at our drive for more (a.k.a. greed), which seems to be one of the primary reasons that contestants turn down smaller cash prizes in hopes that they can win big, even when the odds are one in a thousand.

It should come as no surprise, then, that patience is not easy to practice. As Ambrose Bierce suggests, "Patience is a minor form of despair disguised as a virtue."

We are conditioned to wait and to delay rewards, but our natural impulses tell us to seek those rewards now rather than later, whether those rewards take the form of a TV or a big, fat commission check.

It's a Marathon, Not a Sprint

Naturally, most sales professionals care a great deal about their end-of-month or quarterly commissions. After all, that's part of the incentive of selling: the opportunity to earn potentially more than you would in a position with a fixed income. Likewise, most sales departments and companies also care a great deal about the sales that are made each week, each month, and each quarter. And while long-term projections and future possibilities are good news to company execs, it's more about what is happening right now. The focus and priority is on what sales are coming in today, tomorrow, or next month versus what's possible next year. As a result, sales professionals are incentivized to make sales sooner rather than later, and commission structures are designed to reward the person that closes the sale today.

That's the way the system tends to work.

The short-term thinking is not restricted to the corporate giants and larger companies run by boards and influenced by stockholders. Smaller companies, boutique firms, and even individual sales professionals have absorbed this mind-set and attitude, which is understandable, given that smaller companies and solo sales professionals live or die based on the amount of revenue they have coming through the doors.

It may be understandable, but does it make sense? Does it really increase profits for the long haul?

The traditional sales approach claims to produce immediate results, but not without consequences and fall-out. That is, the emphasis on the immediate sale brings with it certain attitudes, behaviors, expectations, and actions that aren't necessarily positive. The salesperson who feels pressure to close the sale today or this month is going to say and do things to force—or at least encourage—the speed and the likelihood of a sale taking place.

These attitudes and behaviors result in lost sales, dissatisfied customers, or angry prospects who talk (and now blog) about their bad experiences with you and your company. Results like these should not come as a big shock. For if the priority and primary goal is to close sales as quickly as possible, then the focus is on the sales professionals hitting their numbers and the company generating revenue, not on the customer. While this "me first" focus may not impact sales to first-time or unsuspecting customers, it does impact long-term sales potential. At least for sales professionals like Fred. . . .

Just Sign on the Dotted Line for Me

I bet that Fred didn't realize the potential consequences of his decision to use some of the typical sales tactics in an attempt to speed up and close the sale with Natasha. Now he does.

A financial advisor with a nationally recognized firm, Fred was feeling a bit of pressure. Well, a lot of pressure and stress to close more sales and acquire a few more new customers in the fourth quarter. He not only felt that push from his VP, but he wanted to end the year on a high note and qualify for a year-end bonus. So Fred made a decision. He used some of the typical tactics in his attempt to close a sale with Natasha, an account manager for an advertising firm. After meeting Natasha at a casual networking event one night in late October, he called her a number of times in the days following that event, leaving messages on her voice mail about his desire to set up a time to meet.

After returning from vacation, Natasha returned to find his voice mail messages. Unsure of why Fred wanted to meet, Natasha returned his call and inquired about his intentions. Although she had not initially thought to contact Fred about working with him, the timing was right on her end. Fred was in luck, as his call came shortly after Natasha decided it was time to strengthen and expand her financial portfolio.

Interested in learning more, she met with Fred to learn how he might be able to help her. For Fred, Natasha's initial interest must have given him the green light that she was a potential sale to be made before the end of the year. Upon learning this, he recommended a second meeting before the Thanksgiving holiday. She agreed to the meeting, but indicated that she wasn't ready to invest until after the holidays. Focused on his deadlines and feeling pressure to speed up the sale, Fred gave her reasons why she should start working with him sooner rather than later. Which didn't go over so well.

Sensing that Fred wanted to speed up the sale and close on his own timetable, Natasha called him to cancel the second meeting and requested that they reschedule for after the holidays.

Fred never returned her call.

Despite his closing attempts, Natasha was planning on rescheduling that meeting if he had bothered to call her back. And despite her discomfort with his attempts to speed up the sale using the typical tactics, she was willing to give him a second chance. But he never called.

Without hearing from Fred, Natasha is left to assume—and to make up reasons about why Fred didn't call. Chances are good that her assumptions are not going to be favorable. She is left to believe that Fred was "all about Fred" and focused only on his own goals and his need to close more business before the end of the year. Because he put his needs before what was actually best for Natasha (she had told him more than once that January was the best time for her to transfer some investments), he lost the sale and killed any chance of working with her in the future. His actions not only turned her off but prompted her to share her negative experiences with her friends and colleagues, compounding the damage . . . all because Fred chose to move at a speed that was too fast for his prospect.

Fred could have easily saved his reputation and potentially saved the sale with Natasha by adopting the contrarian approach. In doing so, Fred could have returned her call and respected Natasha's wishes to reschedule their meeting for January, the time that worked best for her. With that simple step, Fred could have had a potential sale and the positive regard from an influential member of his local business community.

Then Fred could have used a contrarian strategy to build trust and credibility by sending Natasha relevant articles about investing—or any other information that Natalie would benefit from receiving, such as relevant articles about her industry and her business community. Fred could have quickly built trust and bolstered his reputation by using author Tim Sanders's way of networking—sharing his knowledge, his network, and his compassion—and through keeping in touch by giving away valuable and pitch-free information. Also, Fred could have thought about the fact that Natasha wanted to attract new advertising clients for her company. With that knowledge, he could find ways to help her do that, such as introducing her to other business leaders in his network or by inviting her to a networking event. Additionally, Fred could put together an "Always Have Something to Invite People To" offer that would allow Natasha to build the "know-like-trust" factor with Fred and grow her circle of influence at the same time.

These are simple yet powerful contrarian strategies Fred could have used to create a much different outcome than the one he caused by using the traditional approach.

The Need for Speed

Like Fred, many sales professionals like speed. Speed is a very good thing, but only in the right situation.

In October 1964, Japan introduced the Shinkansen (bullet train) to celebrate and mark the victory of bringing Asia's first Olympic games to Tokyo. A first of its kind, the Japanese high-speed train proved that there was not only a fascination with speed but a market for fast trains. Less than 10 years later, France debuted its TGV high-speed train. Now, there are more than 350 high-speed trains across the globe, including Australia's Speedrail

TGV, which achieves top speeds of up to 360 kilometers per hour (225 miles per hour). Best known for its superfast trains, Japan has the fastest train, which achieves maximum speeds of 552 kilometers per hour (345 miles per hour).

Speed is something we want (and even demand) when it comes to transportation. Well, transportation and a lot of other things.

In the age of fast food, instantly downloadable music, and on-demand everything, faster certainly seems to be better. So much better that consumers will pay top dollar for faster and better everything.

Fed up with dial-up? Just get broadband.

Don't want to drive to Blockbuster? Just order on-demand movies.

Don't have the time to cook real oatmeal? Microwave some instant instead.

Faster certainly seems better. But only when the customer says it is.

With a culture seemingly obsessed with speed, it should come as no surprise to hear that the sales world also embraces the "faster is better" approach to things. There are countless articles on the best way to speed up the sales cycle, accelerate your sales, and fast-forward your prospects to commit with various closing sequences. Faster sales mean more money now—for the company and for the sales professional. Given that profitability is essential to the success of every company, big and small, sales do need to happen sooner rather than later. But how fast is too fast?

Just ask your prospects and customers. They will tell you in no uncertain terms when, where, how, and to what degree they want to engage with you and your products or services. They give you clues about the best way to serve them. And they give you subtle and not-so-subtle feedback when you try to speed things up. Sales professionals who attempt to close the sale as quickly as possible are likely to push the sale at a pace much faster than the customer intends to go.

That was certainly the case when Rob Thomas went to visit a Mazda dealership in Clearwater, Florida.

After spending several days researching different makes and models, Rob was almost ready to purchase a Mazda M3. Although he liked the Toyota Prius, he liked the look and the feel of the Mazda equally well. And it better fit his budget. Like most savvy customers, he had done his research ahead of time. He knew all the features and benefits of the M3 as well as the questions and concerns that had to be addressed by the salesperson before he was willing to buy. He knew when he wanted to buy the car: within the next several days, but not today.

So Rob paid a visit to his local Mazda dealer. That's where he met Phil.

Phil, the Mazda salesman, was friendly at first, but then quickly became too pushy for Rob's tastes. After answering Rob's questions about the Mazda M3, Phil began introducing various preclose questions in hopes that Rob would choose to buy the car right on the spot:

If I can find a price that you are happy with, will you drive one of our cars off the lot today?

Phil asked that question in a number of different ways in order to secure the sale. Instead of closing a sale, Phil managed to frustrate Rob to the point that he left the dealership without a car—and without a desire to return to buy the car from Phil.

What Phil doesn't know is that Rob drove immediately to a Toyota dealership where he met with Sam to discuss buying a Prius. In the end, Rob bought a Toyota Prius, a car that was $150 more per month than the Mazda M3. Because Sam let Rob drive the sale on his own terms, he earned his trust and his sale that same day.

What Phil also doesn't know is that he not only lost a future sale, but he lost many future sales to Rob and Rob's family and friends. Phil could have had the sale, but killed it because he didn't listen to and observe how Rob, the customer, wanted things to go.

Do You Want Fries with That?

Perhaps Phil forgets that he sells cars and not French fries.

At a McDonald's or Starbucks, Phil's desire to push for a quick sale would not only be applauded but encouraged. In the fast-food business, quick and no-hassle sales are an important part of creating the "fast" environment the customer seeks.

In this context, Phil could even politely pressure customers to order fries with their burger or add a muffin to that tall latte without much consequence and without killing sales. Rob can buy the bran muffin for $1.95 with minimal risk. Even if he decides he doesn't want the muffin 10 minutes after buying it, there's very little lost. He can either save the muffin for later or give it to a coworker in the cube next to him. Phil's pressure on Rob to buy more creates little or no ill effect, since spending $1.95 is not something that requires much time or consideration. It's a decision that Rob can make quickly and even compulsively.

The speed at which Rob likes to buy his latte and muffin, however, is probably not the same speed at which he is comfortable buying a car. And that's the big mistake that Phil and others like him make when they try to sell big-ticket items or high-value services at the pace you would sell a burger and fries.

Phil would know exactly how Rob likes to buy if he shifted his focus on the selling process to a focus on Rob's buying process. If Phil asked, Rob would let him know whether he's a compulsive buyer, vulnerable to typical tactics, and thus the guy who typically wants to drive the car off the lot that same day, or whether he's an educated buyer, who needs time to make a decision to buy and wants to work with the "right" salesperson.

Because Phil insisted on controlling the sale, he managed to frustrate Rob. Because of that pressure, Rob actually told Phil that he was not ready to buy that day, which was not true. Rob just didn't want to buy that day from Phil.

Right on Time

Additionally, Phil may not realize that when he attempts to control the sale and speed it up on his terms, he will most likely be out of sync with the customer's natural timing, which is the most critical factor in determining whether he makes a successful sale or creates a big mess. Timing, after all, is everything.

For the comedian . . .
The right timing means the difference between an awkward silence and a crowd that erupts in laughter.

For the farmer . . .

The right time to plant means the difference between a barren field and a bountiful harvest.

For the investor . . .

The right time to sell means the difference between a healthy profit and a devastating loss.

And so it is in sales. Timing can make the difference between a positive selling experience, for both the salesperson and the customer, and a sales nightmare.

So, when is the right time to deliver the punch line, plant the crops, or sell the stock? The comedian, the farmer, and the investor all must study, observe, look, and listen for clues about when the timing is right. Similarly, the salesperson must look for indicators, signs, and clues from the potential customer about when a customer is ready to buy.

As we saw with Phil, the old methods are structured around a different set of priorities and a different sense of timing—that of the salesperson and the company she represents. Almost always, the priorities of the salesperson and the company, as well as the timing around which they want to achieve those priorities, is at odds or in direct conflict with those of the potential client or customer. In choosing to use the traditional tactics, you make a decision. You cannot honor and respect the timing of your customer while using traditional tactics, because they are almost always out of sync with one another.

What's a Boy to Do?

"Take the contrarian approach? It's challenging enough to keep up with what I already know and to implement the conventional daily actions needed to reach potential clients," retorts the experienced sales guy.

In addition to being afraid of trying something new, it's also understandable that sales professionals like you may struggle to take the daily actions to connect with new customers and to follow up with existing ones. Sales folks are notorious for alternating between bursts of sales activity and low periods of inconsistent or no activity. Given this reality, advocates of the conventional strategies believe they provide a stability and consistency needed in the turbulent world of selling—even if that stability is an illusion.

Whether your goal is to be the top salesperson in your organization or to sell just enough not to be fired, routine is important. In fact, the world's top performers confirm the importance of consistency and structure to a winning record. Daily routines are critical to the success of the Olympic gold medalist, the Van Cliburn International Piano Competition winner, and the Oscar-winning actor. The common denominator behind these successes is the willingness and dedication to train intensely, to screen out distractions, and to focus, focus, focus.

On the surface, it seems that the old-school strategies save time, cut down on confusion, and keep the sales professionals focused. They appear to be the best way not only to keep veteran salespeople on track but to train new salespeople as well. Because, at the end of the day, it's only the numbers that matter. Right? Right. . . .

One Size Fits All

In order to keep sales professionals on track, companies craft a specific and detailed training program designed to promote the use of the typical tactics and the traditional sales approach. Whether the training lasts one week or three, it usually ends up costing the company a pretty penny, since even the smallest training sessions require tremendous amounts of time, money, and resources. At a minimum, these training programs include instruction on the company, on the industry, and on the way to sell the company services. This compact training regimen appears to be successful precisely because it uses and relies upon many of the generic strategies that can work "with anyone and in any situation"—based on a faulty belief that all customers are "basically the same."

It doesn't matter whether you are new to sales or are an experienced professional from another firm. Everyone goes through the training program, so there is no question or confusion about the activities expected from you on a daily basis. Too bad that knowing the activities that are expected of you and actually implementing them well are two totally different ball games.

Not familiar with the industry? Not to worry. The training provides an overview of the industry and the basics you need to know before jumping on the phone to make cold calls or going out into the field. In fact, the training program may use various scripts and calling guides so that you should *know* what to say on a voice-mail messages and how to talk to a client about your product or service.

By the end of training, the new sales professional is expected to know how to handle potential objections, how to uncover the desires and priorities of the prospect, and how to advance the sale.

With a script and a leads list, the new recruit is supposedly ready and equipped to start producing immediately. For the new sales professional at many firms, there is no question about the level of activity expected from them each day: 100 calls a day. Well, that and a few quality hours on the phone—a hard thing to achieve if you aren't getting a live person on the phone more than a few times a day. Statistically, 100 calls a day means that you may reach five live prospects—who may or may not be good clients.

By using the typical tactics, companies believe they can quickly train a new group of sales professionals in a "systematic and structured" way, theoretically saving company time and money—until a large percentage of those sales professionals either quit or are fired. Those are the results they think are possible according to their calculations and their interpretations of the results. If reality were only that predictable. . . .

Herding Cats

Customers rarely behave as we want or expect them to. They don't pick up the phone at the right time. They don't always return our phone calls or e-mails. They don't decide to buy from us as soon as we would like them to. They don't make decisions like we do or when we do.

Instead of engaging in a power struggle or insisting on being right, back off. Try doing the opposite. Take a contrarian approach and see what happens. Instead of forcing the sale, find a way to build trust and credibility with prospects so that they want to buy from you when they are ready. And create the circumstances that allow you to be there at the moment they decide to buy.

Sam, the Toyota salesman who sold Rob a Prius, understands this. He had the courage to do everything the opposite way. He took the typical tactics we have come to expect from pushy car salespeople and dumped it in favor of the Contrarian Effect.

Unlike Phil, the pushy car guy from the Mazda dealership, Sam came across as a genuine person and expressed real interest in Rob as a human being rather than seeing him as merely a "prospect." Instead of pushing Rob to make a decision on the spot, Sam asked Rob what type of music he liked. Sam was interested in Rob and took steps to communicate with him, which wouldn't have happened if he tried to use the slick sales talk and the sales pitch that Phil used on Rob. Sam understood the importance of connecting with Rob, as opposed to selling the features and benefits of the Prius. As a result, Rob felt an instant rapport and strong affinity for Sam. So much so that he bought the car from Sam on the spot, even though he told Phil that "he only wanted to gather research and test-drive the car."

One of the quickest ways to implement the contrarian approach is to focus on being friendly, authentic, and likeable. It's the biggest reason why Rob chose to buy from Sam. It's also the biggest reason why your customers choose to work with you.

In his book *The Likeability Factor*, Tim Sanders discusses the importance of how we show up in our communication and in our relationships. He also explains that likeability is essential to building trust and credibility.

In his communication with Rob, Sam demonstrated his likeability with Rob by:

- Listening to Rob and asking questions
- Speaking to Rob as he would a friend—instead of using a sales script
- Focusing on the person rather than the potential sale
- Letting Rob control the pace of the sale
- Trusting Rob to tell him when it's time to buy—instead of relying on pre-close questions
- Giving honest and direct responses to Rob's questions—instead of avoiding the hard questions

Sam made the sale by choosing not to sell and allowing Rob to buy instead. As a result, Sam sold a car much faster than he would have otherwise—and because he decided not to use sales scripts, closing questions, or any other typical tactic to push Rob into buying from him.

Just like Apple.

Salespeople at Apple don't use closing techniques or any of the other tactics to force a sale. They don't have to. Instead, Apple has created an environment that encourages its customers to take as long as they want or need before making a purchase. It doesn't matter whether that purchase is a $79 Shuffle or a Mac Pro with all the bells and whistles that will cost you at least $2,499. You can visit the store every day if you like to test out all of Apple's products. In fact, the company wants you to come in and hold the iPhone in your hands, play with the new video iPod, or click around on an Airbook so you can experience what it's like to type e-mails or write a novel on it.

Nothing about the Apple environment creates a sense of false urgency or pressure for the potential customer. Customers know this. That's why they feel comfortable going back again and again to research future purchases, visit with the sales associates, and browse around the store.

In fact, Apple has created such a pleasant, user-friendly environment that potential Apple users and veterans alike want to stop by the store on a Sunday afternoon just to visit with Apple associates and to browse around. It is this customer-focused and pressure-free *experience* that keeps people coming back for more and more and more. Sure, the iPod is a remarkable gadget, but it's about the experience as much as it's about the product itself. That "Apple experience" is the reason that Elizabeth has a PowerBook laptop, a video iPod (which replaced her original Gen 3 iPod), and a Shuffle, and it's the reason that Michael has a MacBook, a Mac Pro desktop, and an iPhone (which he stood in line to buy on the day they went on sale).

Apple understands that the customer decides when and where to buy. The company creates all the right conditions that allow its customers to get comfortable and get to know its products. And Apple has put together a fun, relaxing environment so that it is "right there" when the customer decides to buy, whether that's tomorrow or next year.

Heard It through the Grapevine

The buzz about Apple is overwhelmingly positive, even among those who don't have an iPod or MacBook. Why? Because Apple's fans and customers talk about their experiences with the store and with the products. They post their reviews on their blogs, on discussion boards, and in e-mails to their friends. They show off their iPhones or iPod nanos proudly as they talk about how much they love Apple. As a result, most folks have a positive impression of Apple and perceive it as a good company—the type of company they want to buy from.

It doesn't matter so much whether Jane next door buys from Apple but what Jane *thinks* about Apple and what it would be like to be an Apple customer. Jane may not buy an iPod, but her neighbor might. And Jane's perception of Apple can strongly influence her neighbor's decision to buy from Apple.

Apple knows this. That's why it has embraced the Contrarian Effect. The company understands that there's a direct relationship between the contrarian approach to selling and its stellar reputation among fans and neophytes alike.

Good for Apple. And good for its bottom line.

May Cause Headaches, Dizziness, and Internal Bleeding

Typical Tactics Harm Reputations and Create Unintended Consequences

YOUR POTENTIAL customers have had it. Feeling empowered by endless options and by the ability to screen out unwanted offers and fend off bad behavior committed in the name of sales, they are taking a stand. Instead of staying quiet, they are telling everyone about it—and using a megaphone to do it.

Frustrated with a pushy salesperson or organization? You've got recourse . . . and a public place where you can rant. If you want justice and a place to vent, visit RipoffReport.com, a web site "by consumers, for consumers," where you can fill out a report and detail your complaint for the world to see. As of February 2008, you can browse 306,256 reports (and counting) to discover who's worth doing business with and who's not. Although there are often significant credibility issues with sites like these, it doesn't matter. They do exist and your potential clients know about them. Even if you do nothing wrong, you can still be "called out" on these sites, which is unfortunate (welcome to the world of Web 2.0). But if you are doing something wrong, brace yourself. You can be sure to find yourself on one of these sites sooner or later.

RipoffReport.com is just one of many outlets angry customers can use to fight back and potentially damage the reputations of the offending parties. Want to "out" a bad salesperson or unethical organization? Now there are a million ways to be heard. Post your grievances on your blog, on YouTube, on a user forum, or anywhere else you find other customers like you who will help you spread your story.

Whistle-Blower

That's what Vincent Ferrari decided to become. Frustrated over the treatment he received from the AOL customer service rep when he tried to cancel his account, he decided to fight back. Fortunately, he made the smart decision to record the call with the AOL rep. With proof of the bad behavior right on the recording, he posted the audio for the world to hear. And, boy, did they! MSNBC even picked up the story, giving thousands more potential AOL customers the opportunity to see why they should choose another Internet service provider.

Sure, it's possible that this one particular sales rep at AOL went against company policy with his efforts to discourage Vincent from canceling his account. But it's not likely. Most likely, that customer service rep was just "doing his job" and doing what he's been told to do: Acknowledge the customer's wishes, but do everything you can to save the sale.

Unless you want to end up on MSNBC, on YouTube, or on a popular blogger's site, you might want to think twice before using some of the typical sales tactics. Unless your offer is relevant, timely, and focused on the needs of the customer, you're signing up for a game of Russian roulette. You never know when the average Joe or Jane you're courting as a prospect has an über-successful blog out in cyberspace. As a result, you are not only jeopardizing the immediate sale but risking the loss of future sales, discouraging referrals, and possibly even risking your very reputation without even knowing it.

Unlike Apple, many sales professionals and companies don't see the connection between how you sell today and how you are perceived tomorrow. Nor do they fully understand that what you do in the short term to convert sales and make your numbers can create negative residual effects for years and years to come. When a salesperson, company, or industry uses the typical tactics over and over to speed up sales and force customers to buy before they are ready, it results in a particular perception of the sales professional, company, or industry. Think used-car salespeople, door-to-door peddlers, or snake-oil salespeople. Each individual act builds upon the one before until there's a strong perception or belief in the public eye about your organization or industry. A perception that usually persists whether it's true or not. A perception that's very difficult to change once it's entrenched in the minds and hearts of potential prospects. Because most folks will simply accept the groupthink about what it's like to do business with you or others in your industry without investigating it for themselves.

Of course, the group has a lot to say about you and what you do.

No Man Is an Island

The aggregate, or sum total, of the actions of all the sales professionals who have gone before you does affect how you are perceived before you even greet a potential customer.

If you are a car salesperson . . .
Know that your prospect has heard that "all car salespeople are crooks" and may think you're like that guy from the used car lot.

If you are a Realtor . . .
Realize that your client may believe that "you can't trust a Realtor" and has heard horror stories about shady real estate agents like the ones depicted in David Mamet's *Glengarry Glen Ross*.

If you are in life insurance . . .
Bet on the fact that your customer has heard this Woody Allen quote: "There are worse things in life than death. Have you ever spent an evening with an insurance salesman?" In fact, she's probably heard it more than once (and wonders if it's true about you).

If you are a financial advisor . . .
Know that movies like *Boiler Room* and *Wall Street* negatively affect how your prospects and potential customers feel about you and your industry.

If you are a mortgage broker . . .

Don't underestimate the effects of the subprime mortgage crisis on your ability to win the trust and the business of customers who have only read about it in the papers. Just because they weren't victims of the scandal doesn't mean that they trust you.

If you are a recruiter . . .

Understand that many people think of you as a "head hunter," which is not a term of endearment or a vote of confidence for your industry.

If you are in the business of selling . . .

Know that your prospects are not interested in doing business with you when they receive a postcard addressed to "[Name] or Current Resident."

Before using one of the typical tactics, think twice about what the "group" may say or do in response that will far outweigh any potential benefits of cutting corners and doing it your way.

I Can Quit Anytime

The fan of the typical tactics asks, "What's the big deal about using the typical tactics every now and then, especially when you know you're not the slick, shady sales type personified by pop culture?"

Here's the big deal about using the traditional strategies: Not only do they have the potential to kill sales and harm relationships with customers, but they negatively affect you. Typical tactics have side effects that can impact your own confidence, morale, and integrity over time.

Using pressure tactics just this once or telling a white lie to close that last sale for the month may not significantly impact your integrity of conscience. After all, your boss told you to make one more sale or else. But what is the cumulative effect on you over time of using the typical tactics as part of your way of doing things? What is the effect of using the typical tactics in order to keep your job and make your numbers?

A furniture salesman from Colorado certainly didn't think his daily actions could affect his health until he became increasingly short of breath for no apparent reason or cause. Although he was overweight, he didn't smoke or suffer from exposure to mold or dust. Yet Dr. Cecile Rose diagnosed him with hypersensitivity pneumonitis after looking at his damaged lungs. Fortunately for him, Dr. Rose took a chance and asked him about his eating habits.

"This is a very weird question, but bear with me. Are you around a lot of popcorn?" Dr. Rose inquired.

Shocked, the man replied, "How could you possibly know that about me? I am Mr. Popcorn. I love popcorn."

As it turns out, the Colorado man had a habit of consuming popcorn at least twice a day for more than 10 years. And, as part of his daily ritual, he inhaled the buttery fragrance after opening the bags. Unfortunately, he now knows that the buttery smell is actually heated diacetyl, the chemical responsible for his chronic lung condition and shortness of breath.

According to a *New York Times* article:

Heated diacetyl becomes a vapor and, when inhaled over a long period of time, seems to lead the small airways in the lungs to become swollen and scarred. Sufferers can breathe in deeply, but they have difficulty exhaling. The severe form of the disease is called bronchiolitis obliterans or "popcorn workers' lung," which can be fatal.

To some, Mr. Popcorn's daily habit may seem extreme or excessive. But to him, it seemed to be a regular part of his routine, one that seemingly produced pleasing results and felt comfortable enough that he didn't see a reason to stop or reduce his popcorn consumption over the 10-year period.

Mr. Popcorn's seemingly harmless daily habit of consuming microwave popcorn proved to be nearly fatal.

No doubt he would have thought twice about ingesting popcorn on a daily basis if he had known that the habit would create a series of unforeseen side effects and unintended consequences.

Ignorance, Error, and Immediate Interest

According to the Law of Unintended Consequences, an idea first introduced during the Scottish Enlightenment and later developed by twentieth-century sociologist Robert K. Merton, almost every action generates at least one unintended consequence. In other words, each cause will likely produce more than one effect, one of which may be unforeseen or unintended. And, depending on the action, that additional consequence may be a good thing or a bad thing. While there are positive outcomes, most unforeseen consequences are negative or perverse in nature.

According to Merton, good intentions are not enough to predict or prevent unintended consequences. As part of his research, he identified five potential causes of unintended consequences:

- Ignorance
- Error
- Immediacy of interest
- Basic values
- Self-defeating prophecy

The first three causes, in particular, are relevant to sales and sales professionals in the following ways.

Ignorance. Given that it is nearly impossible to know everything about every subject, lack of knowledge or understanding or interpretation can lead to unforeseen consequences. In other words, even the best intentions can result in negative outcomes. So the sales professional with the noblest of intentions can still produce unintended negative outcomes as a result of using the typical tactics.

Error. Incorrect analysis of a problem often leads to negative outcomes, as does adopting habits or behaviors that may have worked in the past but may not apply to the current situation or be the best way to achieve the intended result. As Neil Rackham discovered during his research for *Spin Selling,* many sales professionals incorrectly conclude that closing tactics are the reasons for sales success, when in fact they do more harm than good.

Immediacy of interest. In a Web article describing Merton's work, economist Rob Norton explains that Merton's third reason refers "to instances in which an individual wants the intended consequence of an action so much that he purposefully chooses to ignore any unintended effects." This includes acting for self-serving reasons or acting with the immediate payoff in mind rather than the long-term interests. As Norton explains, "That type of willful ignorance is very different from true ignorance." This describes what happened to Fred, the financial advisor, who chose to ignore the possible implications of speeding up the sale with Natasha in order to achieve immediate results.

Even in the most ideal circumstances, it is clear that the typical tactics produce one or more negative unintended consequences. They create consequences that impact sales, reduce repeat business, discourage referrals, and affect company reputations. They create consequences that incur time, money, and energy above and beyond the original scope and budget. They create consequences that often detract significantly from sales results, so much so that the time, money, and energy needed to combat the unforeseen side effects outweighs the original benefits of using the tactics.

Here's the rub. Whether the negative unintended consequences come as a result of ignorance and error, as with Mr. Popcorn, or immediate interest, as with the salesperson who wants instant results so much that he ignores the potential negative long-term effects, these undesirable consequences cannot always be controlled and certainly cannot be eliminated entirely.

Thankfully, knowledge, awareness, and experience can help reduce the negative effects created by true ignorance, lack of experience, incomplete data, or incorrect assumptions.

After observing thousands of sales interactions over a 10-year period as part of his research for *Spin Selling,* Rackham is no longer an advocate of closing techniques as a way to increase sales success. He chooses better and more effective ways to serve his clients and allow them to buy.

The Red Pill or the Blue One?

Now that you are fully aware of data documenting the harm of closing techniques, choosing, for example, to continue using closing techniques would be a reflection of immediate interest, Merton's third cause. Choosing to act with knowledge of a laundry list of negative consequences is similar to adopting the behaviors of the recreational drug user. That is, you would be using the closing question tactic with full awareness of some of the documented harmful side effects it causes and with a decision to risk the additional unforeseen consequences in hopes of the receiving the immediate "hit" or payoff that closing appears to produce. While the typical tactics won't scar your lungs like the heated diacetyl, they can have a cumulative effect on your mental and emotional state.

Perhaps you are fatigued from the never-ending regimen of 100 calls per day. Perhaps you are worn out from calling a list of prospects who don't want to hear from you—and often let you know that fact. Perhaps it's the slimy feeling you get when you tell a slight fib or use a closing technique to convince a prospect to take the next step in working with you because you're under the gun to make sales.

Maybe it's the pressure you feel to make your numbers and to hit certain goals, despite the reality that most prospects don't seem interested or willing to buy right now. Maybe it's the corporate culture, which favors company profits and short-term wins over long-term success and lasting relationships. Maybe it's the high turnover, the "revolving door effect," that serves as a constant reminder that you have to make your month-end numbers—or else. Regular doses of the conventional way of selling may be impacting your physical health, your attitude, your emotional well-being, your confidence, and the way you see yourself. Is it worth using the traditional approach at the expense of your health and overall happiness—just to make a quick buck and instant sale? We think not.

Many sales professionals are not required to use the typical tactics. Hopefully that is the case for you.

Whether you work for a sales organization with lots of rules or one with few to no guidelines, you do have a choice in how you behave. You can choose to use the traditional sales approach or you can decide to be a contrarian. You decide whether to push for the immediate sale or to do what's best both your customer and for your long-term success. You get to determine whether to tolerate the potential side effects of the typical tactics or to put yourself and your customers first.

That's What Makes the World Go Round

"Dream on," says the veteran sales professional who relies on the typical tactics to produce sales. "Everyone knows that sales are all that matter. It doesn't matter how you get there, only that you do."

The sales professionals working for a company that advocates the typical tactics may want to sell differently but feel they have little or no choice in how they make their sales. With the fierce competition all around and their job security on the line, the bottom line is what matters.

This should come as no surprise, given that the main objective for a publicly held company is to find ways to make the share price and value go up. Many companies live and die over whether stock prices and overall metrics are increasing from quarter to quarter. And while companies can cut costs, reduce infrastructure, or lay off employees to boost profits, the market usually frowns on this type of behavior. As a result, the burden of quarterly growth falls on the shoulders of the sales department.

This focus on and desire for short-term profits and immediate sales is certainly not confined to publicly held companies. Rather, it is a reality that extends to privately held companies, smaller firms, and solo entrepreneurs. Call it globalization, increased competition, or the inherent human desire for more, but smaller companies and entrepreneurs want their piece of the pie as well. Why?

Making a sale today is more than simply focusing on sales growth or increasing shareholder value. The drive to make something happen today goes deeper than that. It's about the desire within every sales professional to win. Closing a sale today means that you not only satisfy a customer's needs and earn a commission but that you can experience victory and the satisfaction of a job well done. In a world where competition is fierce and the playing field has been flattened, as described in Thomas Friedman's book, *The World Is Flat*, it pays to make a win as soon as possible. Because every sales professional knows this to be true: There are winners and losers in the game of sales.

Winners and Losers

According to Gregory F. Christiano, the 1950s were a great time to be a kid. For Christiano and his neighborhood pals growing up in the Bronx, the world was their playground—literally. Instead of sitting in front of TV sets to play Xbox and PlayStation, the kids who lived around 184th Street between Washington and Park Avenues played street games, the kind that all his friends knew and loved. As Christiano explains, they could create, play, and compete in an infinite number of ways:

~

We made use of the walls, the stoops, courtyards, sidewalks, curbs, sewers, manhole covers, parked cars, lampposts, fire hydrants, even the red fire alarm box at the corner! Everything on the block had potential; nothing was untouchable and became an integral part of play.

While there were no rulebooks to read or referees to declare a winner, all the kids knew how to play. And they knew who won and who lost. If your pal shouted, "Last one to the stoop is a rotten egg," then you knew you had just lost the game of "Foot Race." If you lost, you could always call for a "Do Over," which meant you had another shot to win the point or win the game. Winning is important, whether you're the kid from 184th Street or the sales professional who wants to be the best on your block.

Since everyone wants to win, it's understandable that big companies and small firms alike are not interested in building relationships and growing long-term opportunities at the expense of short-term profits and immediate wins. After all, today's sales and successes mean that you can stay ahead of the competition and maintain market share.

But is winning by using the traditional sales approach really the best way? NCR president John Patterson decided to win by crushing his competition any way he could. That decision resulted in a one-year jail sentence for antitrust violations. Phil, the Mazda car salesman, tried to win by speeding up the sale, and it backfired, since Rob left the dealership and bought a Prius instead. While winning is important, it *does* matter how you get there.

How can you win in a way that doesn't harm the customer or create negative side effects in the process? How can you win in a way that doesn't sacrifice your long-term potential or your reputation for a sale in the moment?

Pushing Rocks Up a Mountain

"But it's nearly impossible to win when it requires doing something akin to pushing rocks up a mountain," says the advocate of the old-school strategies.

In Greek mythology, there's a myth about a god named Sisyphus. The son of Aeolus, King of Thessaly, and Enarete, Sisyphus had a reputation among the gods as being a big troublemaker. He was known for robbing and murdering travelers along the roads in Corinth. He betrayed the secrets of the gods and even chained up the god of death, Thanatos, preventing Thanatos from reaching the underworld. Fed up with his antics, Hades intervened and inflicted a severe punishment on Sisyphus.

As a penalty for his betrayal, he was banned to the world of the dead and was required to push a rock up a hill—over and over and over again. Once he reached the top of the hill, the law of gravity asserted its influence, causing the rock to roll immediately back down the hill. The pull of gravity on the rock meant that Sisyphus had to go back down the hill to begin his work of pushing the rock up the hill all over again.

From the perspective of the gods, it was the perfect punishment for the one who had betrayed them. Sisyphus had to push the rock up the hill for eternity, never making progress or experiencing one moment of relief from the labor and suffering that came as a result of his punishment. Because the laws of his world meant that the rock would always roll downhill once Sisyphus had pushed it to the top, his efforts made no difference and seemed ultimately futile. No matter how hard he tried, he could not do enough to overcome the law of gravity that counteracted all of his efforts.

Unless you are condemned to a life of endlessly pushing a rock up a hill, you probably won't do it voluntarily. Well, you might try it a few times and then realize that your efforts aren't going to make much of a difference or be strong enough to bend the law of gravity.

Attempting to change the status quo, groupthink, and worldview regarding the typical sales tactics similarly requires effort, focus, and intention, not to mention a different strategy than merely pushing a rock up a hill. Why?

Like it or not, individual sales professionals, sales execs, companies, and consumers have all bought into the "reality" of what sales means, a reality built upon the typical sales tactics. Many customers and sales veterans alike are resigned to believing that closing techniques, pitches, and other strategies used to speed up the sale are just "how things work"—elements that society finds "acceptable" as a means of selling products and services. And, like the law of gravity, many believe that this worldview is extremely difficult, if not impossible, to change.

After all, what's the big deal if you tell white lies about your service so that the prospect will go ahead and buy? It may not be ideal, but that's the way everyone's doing it. . . .

Everyone's Doing It

At any rate, that's what Kyle, the sales associate working for the hardwood floor company Michael contacted, seems to think.

After reading the company's web site and doing some research on its services and offerings, Michael set an appointment with Kyle to clarify some questions he had about the quality of the product and the level of service the company would provide. Although Michael wanted to discuss matters over the phone, Kyle insisted that he visit Michael at his house to better assess his needs.

When Michael asked Kyle about something he had seen on the web site, Kyle explained that "what you see is not always what you get" and that "selling the sizzle" instead of the porterhouse steak (selling less value than you promise) is a common practice:

I want you to understand that what we have printed on the web site is not exactly true. But you can understand . . . that's just marketing. That's how things work.

Because Kyle accepts the typical tactics and traditional paradigm as standard, he couldn't see any problem with his company's posting less-than-accurate information on its web site and with his using that information in an attempt to close more sales. He couldn't see why he wasted Michael's time by coming to his house and trying to sell Michael on the idea that "this is how things work."

Michael's complaints and protests fell on deaf ears, since Kyle didn't conceive of doing things any other way than how they had always been done.

Kyle might have been worried about losing the sale if he thought other hardwood floor retailers had adopted the contrarian way. But he believes that most of them haven't—which is a bet he's making without evidence and without proof that his assumption is really true. But until he gets wind of the company that is doing the opposite, he's not concerned in the least whether his customers agree with "selling the sizzle" to speed up a sale.

As long as everyone else is doing it too, he doesn't have to:

- Feel guilt or have any ill feelings as a result of using the typical tactics
- Consider the implications of using the typical tactics day after day on his customer relationships and on his own well-being
- Worry about changing the status quo (since he believes it's not possible to do so)
- Accept personal responsibility for his actions and consciously choose how he wants to sell

As a sales professional working for a company that operates with the standard paradigm, he believes his responsibility is to sell in the way that his company asks him to and to produce its targeted results. While he may dislike or question the typical way from time to time, he understands the benchmarks he has to hit. And with that, he can quit worrying about whether the typical tactics are the most ethical way of doing things. He can shrug off comments from customers who protest and push back when the typical tactics are used. Right or wrong, that's the system—and he believes his success depends on thriving within that system.

Too bad that Kyle doesn't realize he can play by a different set of rules.

The Full Monty

If you've ever seen the World Series of Poker, then you understand the importance of secrecy. To win the poker game, the players must have skill, the ability to calculate which cards are left in the dealer's deck, and the finesse to cover up or artfully hide their own hand. The player who succeeds in doing this wins.

Unlike the poker champion, the most crafty and secretive salesperson loses big. In the heyday of the typical tactics, keeping secrets and telling little white lies to make a sale may have worked. Not anymore. There's been a big shift in the market—one from secrecy to radical transparency. A shift in which customers want—and require—full disclosure and total honesty.

The customer-driven demand for honesty and full disclosure is another compelling and profitable reason to adopt the contrarian approach. Grounded in a concern for what's best for the customer, even if that means being honest about the limitations of your products or services, the contrarian approach allows you to be radically transparent and open with potential prospects and clients. When you choose to be transparent, customers know it and tell their peers and friends that you're the person to call when it's time to do business.

Radical Transparency

Jay Love knows the benefits of full disclosure and radical transparency. As the founder and CEO of eTapestry.com, he understood that his target market—nonprofits—would more easily trust his company and recognize the benefit of its services by doing the opposite. So Love documented the entire sales cycle and sales process in a downloadable podcast that is available on the company's web site. In doing so, he explains that the eTapestry sales cycle was uniquely designed based on customer feedback and was created to foster relationships—whether a potential client buys or not.

Obviously, the company's strategy is working. As a result of its exponential growth, *Inc.* magazine named it one of the fastest growing companies in 2007. In fact, eTapestry's sales grew so much that Blackbaud, the industry leader, acquired eTapestry in 2007, allowing eTapestry to maintain its sales process and culture as a wholly owned subsidiary.

Like Softrax, eTapestry increased its sales and gained loyal customers as a result of its focus on customer needs and its decision to be radically transparent, an important example for sales professionals, like Kyle, who still resist making a change.

Nothing Less Than the Best

Kyle and others who are afraid of doing the opposite can act like a deer caught in the headlights. Driven by fear of rocking the boat, they cling to the old way, believing they will escape the pain, the loss, and the fallout they will experience if they make a change. In reaction, they do just enough to get by, believing that enough companies will stick to the status quo. Fat chance.

Unlike Kyle, sales professionals wanting to go from good to great or companies wanting to be remarkable understand that *change is inevitable and essential*. The typical tactics can no longer produce a dramatic improvement in sales, since they are the same strategies that created the current reality and that have been used for years. As Albert Einstein observed, "The significant problems we face cannot be solved at the same level of thinking we were at when we created them."

After releasing his wildly successful book, *Permission Marketing,* in 1999, Seth Godin appeared to have hit the top of his game. After all, *Permission Marketing* spent a year on the Amazon Top 100 list and four months on the *BusinessWeek* best-seller list. A runaway hit, the book also appeared on the *New York Times* best-seller list and was named a Fortune Best Business Book.

Then Seth did the unthinkable.

He released his next book, *Unleashing the Ideavirus,* for free. Instead of reaping the rewards and success, Seth did the opposite. He gave his ideas away for free to anyone who went to his web site or to online bookstores, such as Amazon.com, to download a free copy of his e-book.

The risk paid off. *Unleashing the Ideavirus* became the most popular e-book ever written, with more than 2 million people downloading the free digital version. But Seth's success that came as a result of his taking the contrarian approach didn't stop there. Seth went on to publish a hardcover version of the book, which hit number 5 overall on the Amazon best-seller list and was featured in *USA Today* and the *New York Times.*

You can enjoy incredible success and benefit from the long-term payoff that Seth and eTapestry have experienced when you decide to let go of convention and adopt the contrarian approach.

Contrarian Primer

—— ❧ ——

THANKFULLY, many sales professionals and companies before you have taken the contrarian approach and have demonstrated the steps you can take today to achieve the same results. In fact, we offer nine contrarian principles to help you shift your worldview and learn more effective ways to sell.

1. *Build relationships and make connections.*

Each potential customer is human, just like you. He or she is not a "prospect," a "commodity," a "transaction," or a "potential sale." Customers respond best when you engage with them, seek to understand their needs and desires, listen and ask questions, and make a sincere effort to connect with them. Howard Behar, former president of Starbucks Coffee North America and Starbucks Coffee International, knows this. Building relationships and connecting with customers is one of the major reasons that Starbucks has a fiercely loyal following and has become an extremely profitable company. Take Behar's advice: "If you think of your customers as people, you'll make a connection with them, and they'll come back over and over again to enjoy the coffee and the experience."

2. *Respect your customers and honor their wishes.*

From the moment you connect with potential customers, they are in control of the relationship and whether or not it will result in a sale. When you accept that your clients have ultimate control and unlimited choice and that they have the power to speed up or slow down the sale, you honor their wisdom and respect that they know what's best for them. This approach allows you to build trust and credibility quickly, open doors, and earn the right to keep in touch with them over time.

3. *Target specific groups of individuals and the people with whom you do your best work.*

   You can easily and effectively cut through the noise of the marketplace and reach the customers that are meant to buy from you by accepting that not everyone with a pulse and a checkbook is a good—or profitable—client for you. Instead of buying leads lists or attempting to reach the masses, you can sell more by identifying the specific customers and industries that can most benefit from your services. As a result of that knowledge, you can craft very specific and relevant offers for them, speeding up the sales process and establishing long-term relationships with potential clients.

4. *Make relevant and timely offers.*

   When you listen to your target audience, understand their needs and desires, and know why they buy what you are selling, you have a secret weapon that many of your competitors don't have. You have the ability to make valuable and timely offers specifically tailored to your potential clients. Relevancy gives you a sizable advantage, allowing you to follow up frequently and consistently with potential clients so that you are the person they contact when they are ready to buy. It also gives you the specific data you need to put together no-barrier-to-entry offers that give them an experience of what it's like to work with you.

5. *Increase your "likeability factor."*

Customers buy from people they know, like, and trust. They will spend more and want to buy from you if you sincerely demonstrate that you are likable and trustworthy—something that your competitor often forgets. By focusing on the actions that increase the affinity between you and potential customers, sales happen naturally—without any pressure, force, or the need for closing questions.

6. *Practice radical transparency.*

Customers have the power to dig up any information they desire. This reality is a big reason why it pays to practice radical transparency—to be honest, to maintain integrity, and to keep your word. Even though it can be tough to disclose everything fully about you and your product or service, it's the right thing to do. It builds trust with customers and increases the likelihood that they will buy from you—especially if your competitors are telling white lies and fudging the facts. Being transparent is the only way you can build a stellar reputation and be known as *the* person to call when it's time to buy—again and again and again.

7. *Establish yourself as a trusted advisor.*

As Softrax learned as a result of its monthly webinar series, more sales happen when customers see you as a trusted advisor. You can rise to the top of your company or industry when you become an expert on your product or service, fully understand your target market and what they need, and become a reliable resource who offers value regardless of whether clients are ready to buy. As a trusted advisor, clients will seek you out and want to build relationships with you, relationships that result in referrals and repeat business.

8. *Collaborate with strategic partners to leverage your efforts.*

Collaborating with others can mean the difference between meeting quota and having your best year ever. When you strategically partner with others who serve the same market, you not only leverage your efforts, but you reach more potential clients in less time and with less effort— potentials clients who already know and like you as a result of their relationship with your strategic partner. The more qualified clients you have in your network, the more likely you are able to surpass your personal best.

9. *Think bigger about who you are and what you offer your clients.*

You have a special opportunity—the ability to make a difference in the world and to impact powerfully the lives of your customers and clients. Think outside the box and exercise creativity in order to devise new and more effective ways to build relationships and win the hearts and minds of customers. When you build a stable of loyal clients who are motivated to tell everyone about their positive experiences with you, sales automatically happen. Instead of working alone, you have an army of enthusiastic buyers helping you meet potential clients and telling others why they should buy from you. As a result, you have more sales—and the satisfaction of knowing that you make a difference in the world.

Be Like Mike

Grounded in these nine principles, you can quickly and easily implement many of the day-to-day strategies to create a Contrarian Effect.

Be like Royal Canin and . . .
Put together a targeted e-mail program, newsletter, or white paper that provides solutions to the challenges

your customers are facing and gives you an effective way to keep in touch.

Be like Softrax and . . .

Create an "Always Have Something to Invite People To" free offer in the form of a webinar, a teleconference, a brown-bag seminar, or a regular event that brings value to potential clients, builds trust, and gives them an experience of what it's like to buy from you.

Be like eTapestry.com and . . .

Tell potential customers exactly what it's like to work with you. CEO Jay Love outlines the eTapestry.com sales cycle in full on the company's web site so that customers can feel safe in taking the first step in buying its products.

Be like Starbucks and . . .

Focus on relationships so that customers want to buy from you again and again.

Be like Cabela's and . . .

Design an environment that inspires customers to want to hang around you and allows them to buy when they're ready.

Be like Nordstrom and . . .

Put your customers first, even when it means offering refunds with no questions asked.

Be like USAA and . . .

Keep your word and your commitments to your customers so that you have loyal customers—and constant referrals from those loyal customers.

Be like Southwest Airlines and . . .

Do the opposite even when everyone else in your industry is stuck in the status quo. It's the only way you can become the best and sell more than you ever thought possible.

Pendulum Swing

———— ∾ ————

TIGER WOODS IS a contrarian. It's one of the reasons he had the courage to change his golf swing.

Convinced that he could surpass his own personal best, Tiger defied conventional wisdom and expert advice by ditching the swing that helped him achieve stardom in the golf world. In a decision that seemed ludicrous for a man who won the Masters in his first appearance at the tournament and who appeared to be at the top of his game, Tiger abandoned his old swing in favor of a totally different approach. Tiger recognized from the signs—the physical pain and unintended consequences—that his swing had to change in order for him to continue to be the best in the world. In doing so, he fielded harsh criticism from sports writers, reporters, and fans alike. When asked about his decision after missing the cut at the Byron Nelson in May 2005, Tiger offered his defense:

I felt like I could get better. People thought it was asinine for me to change my swing after I won the Masters by 12 shots. . . . Why would you want to change that? Well, I thought I could become better.

Some criticized his decision to leave his swing coach. Others speculated that Woods had simply peaked and was on the decline. The criticism hit a high point in 2004 when Vijay Singh captured the number-one ranking, a spot Tiger had maintained for 264 consecutive weeks.

Just when it seemed that Tiger would have to accept being considered one of the rank and file, the tide turned. In an article for Golf Publisher Syndications, writer Brandon Tucker reported the breakthrough: "After going two full seasons without a major championship, Tiger finally broke through at the Masters in 2005, then claimed the British Open. His No. 1 ranking solidified again."

At the ripe age of 30, Tiger became the youngest player to reach 50 wins. When asked about Tiger's talent, golfing legend Jack Nicklaus predicted that Tiger will win more majors than he or Arnold Palmer won put together. This seems likely, given that Tiger tied Arnold Palmer for fourth place on the all-time PGA Tour winners' list after winning a record sixth Buick Invitational in January 2008. And he's not retiring anytime soon.

With 13 major titles under his belt and the possibility of a Grand Slam on the minds of fans and commentators alike, Tiger's future has never looked brighter.

By making a decision to be a contrarian, Tiger has experienced amazing success because he was willing to endure the *temporary* setbacks that are an inevitable part of making the journey from good to great.

Leader of the Pack

From its inception, Southwest Airlines chose to take the usual approach and do the opposite. Former Southwest CEO James F. Parker describes the attitudes and the approach of Herb Kelleher and Southwest founders in his book, *Do the Right Thing*: "Southwest was not your standard corporate bureaucracy. These were mavericks who were breaking all of the old rules and making new ones." At a time in history when airlines could, thanks to government regulation, charge high prices and provide poor service, Southwest found a way to put the customer first and move ahead of its competition. Due to a legal loophole, Southwest was able to bypass federal regulations and take control over how much it charged and how often it flew. Using California-based PSA airlines as its model, Southwest initially focused on a very specific market, intrastate flights throughout Texas, and a very specific customer, the frequent business traveler.

By offering low-cost fares, frequent flights, and fast, friendly service, Southwest quickly became a customer favorite—and a threat to the competition. Instead of focusing on its airline competitors, the company understood that the automobile was its true competitor and that it had to provide enough value for business travelers to decide to fly instead of drive.

Southwest succeeded—much to its competitors' dismay. Rival airlines Braniff and Texas International Airlines (TIA) did everything they could to stop Southwest and to take back some of the business that Southwest earned. They did everything from suing the company to copying its business model by offering lower fares in an attempt to bankrupt the company.

Southwest withstood the challenge. What Braniff, TIA, and others didn't understand was that Southwest's success was not due to low fares. Sure, the affordable flights attracted customers initially, but Southwest quickly became the market leader because of its focus on the customer and its decision to do the right thing.

In the aftermath of the September 11 attacks, Southwest's customer-centric focus paid off. While other airlines lost millions in revenue and laid off thousands of workers, Southwest remained profitable. Even when company CEO James F. Parker made the decision to offer refunds without penalty and without condition, many loyal Southwest customers chose not to ask for a refund. Southwest's commitment to its employees and customers is the reason the company is more profitable than any other airline.

Parker attributes Southwest's success in part to listening to its customers and understanding why they buy. As he explains, "Customers shop for value, and value involves a combination of price and quality. An enduring competitive advantage comes from consistently and reliably offering customers the best value over an extended period of time." In doing so, the company created a Contrarian Effect—and won the hearts of thousands of loyal customers who buy again and again and who will even go out of their way to fly with Southwest.

Good to Great

Like Tiger and Southwest Airlines, you have an incredible opportunity. You can observe the signals indicating that the usual way won't help you go from good to great and decide to make a change. You can choose to be the best sales professional in your company and in your industry by letting go of the typical tactics in favor of doing the opposite.

Adopting the contrarian way is about selling more. It's about implementing a simple, affordable, easy, and effective way to attract customers and to sell as much as possible. It's about embracing a different worldview and stepping into the new reality that your customers have created—and that they control.

Remember, it's not about being right or wrong. It's about doing the best thing for your customers and being on the right side of reciprocity—while selling as much as possible. When you are focused on your customer, you remove any resistance and force so that sales happen quickly, easily, and naturally. That's the Contrarian Effect.

Doing the right thing and making a difference never felt so good—nor paid so well.

References

―――――― ∾ ――――――

For a complete list of the resources mentioned in this book, along with hundreds of others on how to create the Contrarian Effect, please go to www.TheContrarianEffect .com and choose the Free Resources section for immediate access.

Anderson, Chris. "Sorry PR People: You're Blocked." TheLongTail .com, October 29, 2007.

Behar, Howard, with Janet Goldstein. *It's Not About the Coffee*. New York: Penguin/Portfolio, 2007.

Christiano, Gregory F. "The Games—How We Played Them." www .myrecollection.com/christianog/games.html.

Friedman, Walter A. "John H. Patterson and the Sales Strategy of the National Cash Register Company, 1884 to 1922." *Business History Review*. Boston, 1998.

Godin, Seth. *Permission Marketing*. New York: Simon and Schuster, 1999.

Goldberg, Alan B., and Bill Ritter, "Costco CEO Finds Pro-Worker Means Profitability." ABCNews.com, August 2, 2006.

Harris, Gardiner. "Doctor Links a Man's Illness to a Microwave Popcorn Habit." *New York Times,* September 5, 2007.

Ketchum Public Relations and the University of Southern California Annenberg Strategic Public Relations Center. *Media, Myths and Realities*. Survey conducted among 1,227 adult U.S. citizens from September 30 to October 5, 2007.

Konrath, Jill. "The Buyer's Lament." SellingtoBigCompanies.com article on March 24, 2007.

_____. "The Perfect Pitch—Or Is It?" Sellingto BigCompanies.com blog on October 17, 2006.

Malley, Aidan. "Tracking Down Apple's Missing 1.4m iPhones." AppleInsider.com, January 24, 2008.

McGregor, Jena. "Customer Service Champs." *BusinessWeek,* March 2007.

Merton, Robert K. "The Unanticipated Consequences of Purposive Social Action." *American Sociological Review,* Vol. 1 Issue 6, December 1936: 894–904.

Natsu, Jennifer. "How a Pet Food Company Is Building a Loyal Customer Based via Highly Targeted Emails." MarketingProfs .com (accessed July 31, 2007).

Norton, Rob. "Unintended Consequences," *The Concise Encyclopedia of Economics,* David R. Henderson, ed. Library of Economics and

Liberty. www.econlib.org/library/Enc/UnintendedConsequences
.html (accessed March 14, 2008).

Parker, James F. *Do the Right Thing.* Upper Saddle River, NJ:
Wharton School Publishing, 2008.

Port, Michael. *Book Yourself Solid.* New York: John Wiley & Sons,
2006.

Rackham, Neil. *Spin Selling.* New York: McGraw-Hill, 1988.

Robertson, Morgan. *Wreck of the Titan.* 1898.

Sanders, Tim. *The Likeability Factor.* New York: Crown, 2005.

_____. *Love Is the Killer App.* New York: Three Rivers
Press, 2003.

_____. "Futility," *Pall Mall Gazette.* London, 1886.

Smith, Adam. *An Inquiry into the Nature and Causes of the Wealth of
Nations.* London, March 1776.

Smith, Kimberly. "How a Software Firm's Soft-Sell, Educational
Webcasts Helped Double Sales." MarketingProfs.com (accessed
September 4, 2007).

Stead, William T. *From the Old World to the New.* London: Review of
Reviews, 1892.

Story, Louise. "Anywhere the Eye Can See, It's Likely to See an
Ad." *New York Times,* January 15, 2007.

About the Authors

MICHAEL PORT is the author of *Book Yourself Solid: The Fastest, Easiest, and Most Reliable System for Getting More Clients Than You Can Handle Even If You Hate Marketing and Selling* and *Beyond Booked Solid: Your Business, Your Life, Your Way—It's All Inside*. He's been called a "marketing guru" by the *Wall Street Journal* and is a renowned public speaker. A slightly irreverent, sometimes funny, knowledgeable, compassionate, and passionate performer, Michael hits his mark every time and leaves his audiences, readers, and clients a little smarter, much more alive, and thinking a heck of a lot bigger about who they are and what they offer the world.

Born and bred in Manhattan, Michael now lives in picturesque Bucks County, Pennsylvania, where, when he's not traveling, he enjoys a quieter lifestyle focused on his son, his work, and his martial arts training. You can find him online at www.MichaelPort.com.

Elizabeth Marshall is the Director of Sales for Michael Port Companies and the owner of Marketing Marshall, a marketing and sales firm dedicated to helping sales professionals, business experts, and top authors attract clients, spread their messages, and sell their books. While working in sales at the nationally recognized Merritt, Hawkins and Associates, she was awarded Research Recruiter of the Month five out of her last six months with the company. Additionally, she is the founder of AuthorTeleseminars.com, an online community in which she hosts interviews with top business authors, including Seth Godin, Chris Anderson, Tim Ferriss, Rich Sloan, Dan Pink, and Keith Ferrazzi.

A native Texan, Elizabeth currently resides in Dallas, loves eating Mexican food and sushi, and enjoys great conversation with friends and family. When she is not writing, speaking, or working with clients, she enjoys practicing yoga, watching NBA games, and playing ball with Barkley, her Australian shepherd. You can find her online at www.MarketingMarshall.com and www.Author Teleseminars.com.

Index